1 MONTH OF
FREE
READING

at

www.ForgottenBooks.com

By purchasing this book you are eligible for one month membership to ForgottenBooks.com, giving you unlimited access to our entire collection of over 1,000,000 titles via our web site and mobile apps.

To claim your free month visit:
www.forgottenbooks.com/free891770

* Offer is valid for 45 days from date of purchase. Terms and conditions apply.

ISBN 978-0-266-80254-9
PIBN 10891770

This book is a reproduction of an important historical work. Forgotten Books uses state-of-the-art technology to digitally reconstruct the work, preserving the original format whilst repairing imperfections present in the aged copy. In rare cases, an imperfection in the original, such as a blemish or missing page, may be replicated in our edition. We do, however, repair the vast majority of imperfections successfully; any imperfections that remain are intentionally left to preserve the state of such historical works.

Forgotten Books is a registered trademark of FB &c Ltd.
Copyright © 2018 FB &c Ltd.
FB &c Ltd, Dalton House, 60 Windsor Avenue, London, SW19 2RR.
Company number 08720141. Registered in England and Wales.

For support please visit www.forgottenbooks.com

r Historical Microreproductions / Institut canadien de microreproductions historiques

1998

phic Notes / Notes techniques et bibliographiques

L'Institut a microfilmé le meilleur exemplaire qu'il lui a été possible de se procurer. Les détails de cet exemplaire qui sont peut-être uniques du point de vue bibliographique, qui peuvent modifier une image reproduite, ou qui peuvent exiger une modification dans la méthode normale de filmage sont indiqués ci-dessous.

☐ Coloured pages / Pages de couleur

☐ Pages damaged / Pages endommagées

☐ Pages restored and/or laminated / Pages restaurées et/ou pelliculées

☑ Pages discoloured, stained or foxed / Pages décolorées, tachetées ou piquées

☐ Pages detached / Pages détachées

☑ Showthrough / Transparence

☐ Quality of print varies / Qualité inégale de l'impression

☐ Includes supplementary material / Comprend du matériel supplémentaire

☐ Pages wholly or partially obscured by errata slips, tissues, etc., have been refilmed to ensure the best possible image / Les pages totalement ou partiellement obscurcies par un feuillet d'errata, une pelure, etc., ont été filmées à nouveau de façon à obtenir la meilleure image possible.

☐ Opposing pages with varying colouration or discolourations are filmed twice to ensure the best possible image / Les pages s'opposant ayant des colorations variables ou des décolorations sont filmées deux fois afin d'obtenir la meilleure image possible.

L'exemplaire filmé fut reproduit grâce à la générosité de:

University of Alberta
Edmonton

Les images suivantes ont été reproduites avec le plus grand soin, compte tenu de la condition et de la netteté de l'exemplaire filmé, et en conformité avec les conditions du contrat de filmage.

Les exemplaires originaux dont la couverture en papier est imprimée sont filmés en commençant par le premier plat et en terminant soit par la dernière page qui comporte une empreinte d'impression ou d'illustration, soit par le second plat, selon le cas. Tous les autres exemplaires originaux sont filmés en commençant par la première page qui comporte une empreinte d'impression ou d'illustration et en terminant par la dernière page qui comporte une telle empreinte.

Un des symboles suivants apparaîtra sur la dernière image de chaque microfiche, selon le cas: le symbole ⟶ signifie "A SUIVRE", le symbole ▽ signifie "FIN".

Les cartes, planches, tableaux, etc., peuvent être filmés à des taux de réduction différents. Lorsque le document est trop grand pour être reproduit en un seul cliché, il est filmé à partir de l'angle supérieur gauche, de gauche à droite, et de haut en bas, en prenant le nombre d'images nécessaire. Les diagrammes suivants illustrent la méthode.

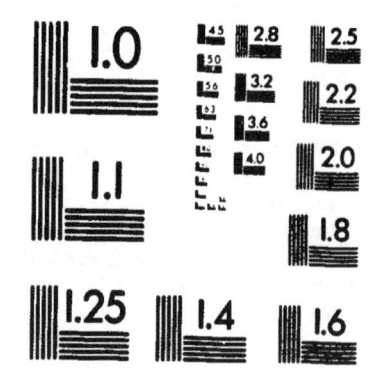

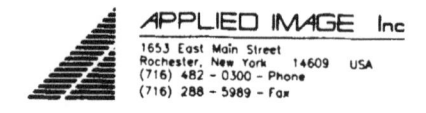

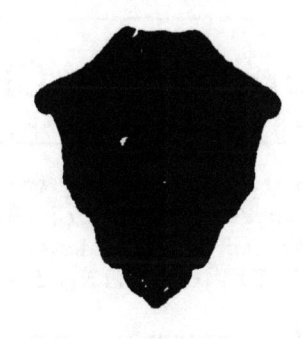

Souvenirs of the Chateau
MAY BE OBTAINED AT THE COUNTER

¶ Visitors should not fail to procure some of these Souvenirs. They are intrinsically interesting and valuable, and are sold for the BENEFIT OF THE CHATEAU

WM. ST. PIERRE

Ladies' and Gentlemen's High Class Tailors

41-43 UNION AVE., MONTREAL

JAEGER *Overwear and Underwear*

Known wherever clothes are worn.

TRAVELLERS' SPECIALTIES

JAEGER pure wool world famous underwear All weights and sizes—guaranteed against shrinkage.

JAEGER pure wool and camelhair travelling rugs.

JAEGER sweater coats for men and ladies.

JAEGER pure wool and camelhair dressing gowns.

JAEGER motor coats and ulsters.

The Jaeger Store at 316 St. Catherine Street West (near Birks' Jewelry Store) is a place of interest to American and other travellers and tourists.

Dr. JAEGER SANITARY WOOLLEN SYSTEM Co.
316 St. Catherine Street West, MONTREAL

CATALOGUE

OF THE

Chateau de Ramezay

Museum and Portrait Gallery

Prepared by
THOMAS O'LEARY
Assistant Librarian
(Under the supervision of the President of the Antiquarian Society)

EIGHTH EDITION

MONTREAL, 1912

CHATEAU DE RAMEZAY

The Chateau de Ramezay

Claude de Ramezay, eleventh Governor of Montreal, appointed 1703, was born in France 1657, came to Canada in 1685, with a number of other young officers, in the suite of Governor de Denonville. He was then a lieutenant in de Troye's company of Marine troops, which later took part in the expedition to Hudson's Bay. His promotion was rapid, being captain in 1687, later colonel, then commandant of troops and finally Governor of the Town and its district.

In 1687 he took part in the expedition against the Iroquois and in 1690, when Phipps appeared before Quebec, he brought over 800 men from Montreal for the defence of the former town.

History tells of the spirited defence made by Frontenac and his gallant officers, the latter, no doubt, being encouraged by the bright smiles of some of Quebec's fair daughters who it seems, lost no time in rewarding their brave defenders with their heart and hand. Scarcely had the last of Phipp's fleet disappeared around Point Levi, than de Ramesay led to the altar Melle Marie-Charlotte Denys, a daughter of Denys de la Ronde, one of the wealthiest families of Canada. His companion in arms, de Vaudreuil, at the same time married Louise daughter of Pierre de Joybert de Soulanges. Could they have seen into the future their happiness would have been clouded by sorrow, for it was destined that a son of de Ramezay should be the one to o en the gates of Quebec to the English in 1759 and a son of depVaudreuil should do likewise, at Montreal, the following year.

De Ramezay was one of the most prominent men of this time, occupying an official position in Canada for a term exceeding forty years. He was Seigneur de la Gesse, de Montigny, et Boisfleurent in France, and in Canada was Seigneur de Monnoir and de Ramezay, Knight of the Military Order of St. Louis, Governor of Montreal, and Commandant of all the militia in the country, and was administrator of the Governor-Generalship during the two years' absence of de Vaudreuil in France.

The Chateau was built in 1705. The neighborhood was then the fashionable part of the town, and was occupied by the Baron de Longueuil, the Contrecoeurs, d'Eschambaults, d'Aillebousts and Madame de Portneuf, the widow of Baron

Becancourt. Situated on a hill, and opposite to the magnificent garden of the Jesuits, this plain unembellished house had an open view to the river front. The vaults were of ancient castle construction. Even the attic floors were of stone slabs.

Under de Ramesay's regime, 1703 to 1724, this venerable edifice was the hall of entertainment of the illustrious of the country. The many expeditions to the distant fur fields, the voyages of discovery of new lands, the councils of war, the military expeditions, the conferences with the Indians, the annual fairs and fur trading market, attracted to the shores of Montreal, not only the Governor-General, the Intendant, and their suites, but a considerable number of the most important people of the country, including all classes of society. To one and all the portals of this hospitable mansion were ever open. To the lowly Indian and his squaw, and to the exalted nobleman and his consort, the noble and beneficient Ramesay and his family showed equal attention. Fearless to the Indian or enemy, his bravery and charity were equally exemplified in the personal care and attention he and his family gave to the suffering citizens of Montreal during the pest which devastated the town in 1721.

De Ramesay died in 1724, and his family sold the Chateau to the *Compagnie des Indes* in 1745. The latter retained possession until the cession, in 1763, when it was bought by Wm. Grant, who, in turn, disposed of it to the English Government for the sum of two thousand guineas. It thus became again the residence of the Governors, and remained such up to 1849.

In 1775-6, the Chateau was the Headquarters for the Continental Army under Montgomery, and in the spring of 1776, there came Benjamin Franklin, Carroll of Carrollton, and Samuel Chase, envoys sent by Congress to influence the French Canadians to join the colonies in the revolt against British rule. Then came Benedict Arnold, who occupied the Chateau for several weeks. The mark of the old reception dais is still seen on the salon walls.

Lord Metcalfe was the last resident governor, but for some years after his establishment in a new government house the Chateau was used for departmental offices. When the government was withdrawn from Montreal, the Chateau served several purposes. For some years courts were held here, and later the Normal School, then courts again.

In 1894 the Chateau was sold by the Provincial Government and purchased by the Corporation of the City of Montreal, for the Numismatic and Antiquarian Society which in 1895, obtained the building for the purpose of founding their Historical Portrait Gallery and Museum.

The Antiquarian and Numismatic Society of Montreal

In the month of December, 1862, several gentlemen of Montreal, desirous of cultivating the study of Numismatics, some of whom had been meeting informally for a couple of years at the house of Mr. James Ferrier, judging the formation of a properly organised association as the most efficacious means of attaining that end, formed "The Numismatic Society of Montreal." The seal of this society was the obverse of the Canadian bronze cent, with an outer circle inscribed "Societe Numismatique de Montreal. Fondee 1862."

In January, 1866, the name of the society was changed to that of the "Numismatic and Antiquarian Society of Montreal," and a new seal was adopted, viz.: a round shield quartered by a tomahawk, and calumet, bearing an antique lamp, an Athenian coin with the head of Minerva, a Canadian cent with head of Victoria and a Beaver; the shield encircled with a garter bearing the words: "Numismaticae et Archelogicae Marianopolitanae Societatis Sigillum."

In 1912 the charter of incorporation was amended by Act of the Provincial Legislature and the name of the Society changed to "The Antiquarian and Numismatic Society of Montreal."

In July, 1872, the Society began the publication of "The Canadian Antiquarian and Numismatic Journal." Up to the present time three series, making a total of twenty-four volumes have been published. It was this Society, acting upon the projects of individual members of it, that first suggested the project of celebrating the 250th anniversary of the founding of Montreal, and proposed three things in order to shed more lustre on so noteworthy an event. First, the erecting of a monument to the memory of Chomedy de Maisonneuve, the founder of our city; second, the saving of the Chateau de Ramesay from the destruction with which it was threatened; third, an historical exhibition by which the public might be enlightened regarding the rare and precious things still to be found amongst us and which the Society is endeavoring to prevent being lost to the country for ever.

The Society succeeded in bringing all three of these projects to a successful issue, and the results of its labors in the Chateau may be read in the pages of this catalogue.

PATRON
H. R. H. THE DUKE OF CONNAUGHT.
GOVERNOR-GENERAL OF CANADA.

PRESIDENT
W. D. LIGHTHALL, ESQ., K. C.

VICE-PRESIDENTS

JUDGE EUG. LAFONTAINE	CHS. T. HART, ESQ.
LUDGER GRAVEL, ESQ.	JAS. REID, ESQ.
REV. ABBE N. DUBOIS	S. M. BAYLIS, ESQ.

HON. TREASURER   HON. RECORDING SECRETARY
GEORGE DURNFORD, ESQ.   C. A. HARWOOD, ESQ. K.C.

HON. CURATOR
R. W. MC'LACHLAN, ESQ. F. R. S. C.

HON. CORRESPONDING SECRETARY
PEMBERTON SMITH, ESQ.

HON. LIBRARIAN
ALD. VICTOR MORIN, ESQ. N. P.

COUNCIL

J. C. A. HERIOT, ESQ.	A. CHAUSSE, ESQ.
R. PINKERTON, ESQ.	P. O. TREMBLAY, ESQ.
S. W. EWING, ESQ.	G. N. MONCEL, ESQ.
O. M. H. LAPALICE, ESQ.	P. J. L'HEUREUX, ESQ.
E. Z. MASSICOTTE, ESQ.	

ASSISTANT LIBRARIAN
MR. THOS. O'LEARY.

CATALOGUE

HALL.

PAINTINGS, ENGRAVINGS, PHOTOGRAVURES, ETC.

(The names of the donors are printed in italics.)

1. The first Ursuline Monastery in Quebec, built in 1640 destroyed by fire in 1641. Very old oil painting copied from the original in the Ursuline Convent, Quebec. The house in the foreground belonged to Madame de la Peltrie, the foundress, and was occupied by Bishop Laval upon his arrival, 1659. *Oil.*
    Mrs. S. E. McDonald.

2. Ruins of Fort Senneville. Built by Jacques Le Ber de Senneville in 1697. Dismantled by the Americans by order of Benedict Arnold, in 1775. *Photo.*

3. The Manor House of Jacques Cartier, at Portneuf painted on the spot in 1889 by J. C. Franchere. *Oil.*
    By Purchase.

4. Carte du Canada, ou Nouvelle France, 1732.

5. L'Amerique Septemtrionale, 1730.

6. Partie Orientale du Canada, 1775.
    S. Carsley, Esq.

7. Carte de la Nouvelle France, 1690.
    H. J. Tiffin, Esq.

8. Haldimand Castle, Quebec. Built by Governor Haldimand, in 1784, in the south-west angle of the Old Fort built by Frontenac in 1692. Demolished, 1892, to give place to the Chateau Frontenac Hotel. *Oil.*

9. The Intendant's Palace, Quebec, in 1759. Destroyed by shells fired from the Ramparts to dislodge the Americans who had taken possession of it, under Benedict Arnold, in 1775. The vaults are now used by Boswell Bros., brewers. *Water color.*
    H. J. Tiffin, Esq.

10. The Chateau de Longueuil, built by LeMoyne de Longueuil in 1685, destroyed by fire in 1792. Occupied by Americans in 1775. *Water color.*
    Hon. Judge Baby.

11. Fort Senneville. Built in 1697, by Jacques Le Ber de Senneville. Attacked in 1747 by the Mohawks. Dismantled by the American troops, by order of Benedict Arnold, 1775. *Water color.*
George Durnford, Esq.

12. Old Fort Chambly in 1886. Fort Chambly was attacked and captured by General Montgomery, Oct. 18, 1775. *Water color.* *H. C. Nelson, Esq.*

13. Ruins of the "Capitulation House," Cote des Neiges road, sketch made in 1889. It was in this house that the capitulation of Montreal is supposed to have been signed, Sept. 8, 1760. *Water color.*
R. W. McLachlan, Esq.

14. View of the Old Convent, Nun's Island. *Photo.*
Hon. Judge Baby.

15. Trafalgar Tower, Cote-des-Neiges Road. *Water color.*
J. H. Ross, Esq.

16. View of old Canadian house at Fraserville, formerly used as a summer hotel. *Photo.*
George Durnford, Esq.

17. Simon Fraser cottage at St. Anne de Bellevue in which Thomas Moore, the poet, resided about 1806. *Water color.* *J. H. Ross, Esq.*

18. The Cuthbert Chapel at Berthier, built by the Hon. James Cuthbert. The first Protestant chapel built after the conquest of New France, 1786. *Water color.*
Dr. Mackenzie Forbes.

19. The Manor House, St.-Jean Port Joli. *Photo.*

20. The Manor House, Fraserville. *Photo.*

21. The second St. Patrick's Church at Riviere-du-Loup, built in 1812, demolished in 1856. *Photo.*
Chas. T. Hart, Esq.

22-23. Two views of the City of Ottawa, drawn in 1855, by E. Whitefield. *Colored lithograph.*

24. View of the City of Kingston, in 1855, by E. Whitefield. *Colored lithograph.* *Hon. Judge Baby.*

25. Montreal. Seven Oaks, Kent. The seat of the Right Hon. the Earl of Amherst. *Photo.*

26. The Obelisk, Montreal Park, Seven Oaks, Kent, Eng., in memory of Gen. Amherst. *Photo.*
Rt. Hon. Earl Amherst, through W. D. Lighthall, K.C.

27. Photographs of the bronze tablets on the monument at Pointe-a-Callière, bearing the names of the first settlers of Montreal. *J. A. U. Beaudry, Esq.*

28. View of the City of Toronto, drawn in 1855, by E. Whitefield. *Colored lithograph.*
J. Ross-Robertson, Esq.

ELGIN GALLERY.

This Portrait Gallery is named in honor of the Right Honorable the Earl of Elgin, who used the Chateau Offices in 1849.

PORTRAITS.

1. Bienville, Jean-Baptiste Le Moyne de, born 1680, died in France, 1768. Governor of Louisiana twenty-seven years. (See 2, 3, and Antiquities 88, 89.) Founded New Orleans 1717. *Oil.* *By Subscription.*

2. De Longueuil, Charles Le Moyne, Baron, born 1657, died 1729. Son of Charles Le Moyne, Sieur de Longueuil. Created baron 1700, had great influence over the Indians, served in Flanders as aide-de-camp to Marshal d'Humieres; governor of Detroit 1700, and later governor of Montreal. *Oil.*

3. D'Iberville, Pierre Le Moyne, Sieur, born 1661, died 1706, in the West Indies, his body resting in the Cathedral of Havana, Cuba. Founder and First Governor of Louisiana, a brother of Bienville and of the first Baron de Longueuil. Entered the marine at an early age and became a noted sea fighter; took Fort Nelson in Hudson's Bay. Discovered the mouth of the Mississippi. *Oil.*

Donor of 1, 2 and 3. Charles Colmore Grant, 7th Baron de Longueuil.

4. Lanaudiere, Charles Tarieu de, born 1741, died 1811; was a great-grandson of Claude de Ramezay, who built the Chateau. Entered the army and was wounded in the battle of the Plains of Abraham, being then *Aide Major* in the Regiment of La Sarre, although barely sixteen years of age. Went to France after the capitulation of Montreal. Returned to Canada a few years later, when he married Melle. Lacorne de St. Luc. Aide-de-camp to Lord Dorchester in 1775, he contributed not a little to save him from falling into the hands of the *Bostonais*. Was with Bourgoyne's army and called

upon, together with his father-in-law, Lacorne, to appear before the Committee of the House of Commons appointed to investigate the conduct of the general. *Oil.*
Wm. Selby, Esq.

5. Lacorne St. Luc, Luc de Chapt de. Knight of the Order of St. Louis. Montcalm's General of Indians. Took Fort Clinton in 1747. Was present at Carillon and at St. Foy. After the conquest he emigrated, but saved himself from the wreck of the ship "l'Auguste," in the Gulf, and remained in Canada. An Executive Councillor under the new regime. Fought at St. Johns, and accompanied Bourgoyne with a command of Canadians and Indians. *Oil.* (See 4, 29 and 136.)
Archbishopric, Montreal.

6. De Levis, Chevalier, born 1720, died 1787. Second in command under Montcalm. He took part at the battle of Ticonderoga, where he commanded the right division, as also at Montmorency, where the French repulsed Wolfe. He was absent at Montreal when the first battle of Quebec was fought. At the second battle of of Quebec defeated Murray. *Oil.*
Marquis de Levis, France.

7. Talon, Jean. Comte d'Orsainville, the great Intendant of the French Government in Canada. Appointed 1663. *Oil.*
By Subscription.

8. Champlain, Samuel de, born 1567, died 1635. The Father of New France and founder of Quebec. *Oil.* Made up from the Montcornet Portrait.
H. J. Tiffin, Esq.

9. Imbert. A member of the Supreme Council of Quebec. Returned to France in 1760. *Oil.*
Archbishopric, Montreal.

10. Youville, Francois-Madeleine, You d', Sieur de la Decouverte, officer, born 1700, died 1730. Married Marie-Marguerite Dufrost de la Jemerais, afterwards foundress of the General Hospital and first Superioress of the Grey Nuns. *Oil.* (See 164 to 168.)
By Subscription.

11. De Beaujeu, Daniel-Marie-Hyacinthe-Lienard, born 1711, died in 1755. Chevalier de St. Louis. Commander General of Fort Duquesne and of the army at *Belle l'iviere* (Ohio). Defeated Braddock in the battle of the Monongahela, both being killed on the field, as were, four years later, Wolfe and Montcalm on the Plains of Abraham. *Oil.*
H. J. Tiffin, Esq.

12. Guy, Colonel Pierre, born at Montreal Dec. 11, 1738. died January, 1812. One of the signers of the capitulation of Montreal to Gen. Montgomery in 1775. Was President or member of many important Government Commissions. *Oil.*

13. Baby, Colonel, the Honorable Francois, Adjutant-General of Militia, Lower Canada, member of the Executive and Legislative Councils, deputy of the French-Canadians to the Court of Great Britain in 1773. Born at Montreal, Dec. 4, 1733; married Delle Marie-Anne Tarieu de Lanaudiere, Feb., 1786; died at Quebec, Oct., 1820. (See 34). *Oil.*   *Hon. Judge Baby.*

14. De Salaberry, C. B., Col. Hon. Charles-Michel d'Irumberry, born 1778, died 1820. Called the Hero of Chateauguay. On October 20, 1813, 350 French-Canadian Militia, led by him defeated 3,500 United States troops under General Hampton at Chateauguay, who believed themselves surrounded by a force far superior in numbers. The battle saved Canada at a critical moment of the war. *Oil.* (See 55, 78, 79' 80, 99, 100.)
   By Subscription.

15. Globensky, Lieut.-Colonel Maximilien, born 1793, died 1866. Lieutenant of Voltigeurs, 1812, under de Salaberry. Fought at Ormstown and Lacolle. Captain of a Company of Volunteer Loyalists at St. Eustache, 1837. *Oil*   *C. A. M. Globensky, Esq.*

16. Franchere, Gabriel, a renowned Canadian traveller and explorer, took part in several expeditions to the Pacific by way of Cape Horn to the Sandwich Islands, later he crossed the Rocky Mountains, exploring the country between them and Lake Superior. Published an account of his voyages in 1820, died at St. Paul, Minnesota, 1863. *Lithograph.*

17. Tonnancourt, Louis-Joseph Godfroy de, born 1712, Sub-delegate of the Intendant and Procureur du Roy, at Three Rivers. *Oil.*   *Madame de Tonnancourt.*

18. DeMontigny, Chevalier Jean-Baptiste Testard. Born 1724, died 1786. Knight of St. Louis. Fought at the Monongahela with de Beaujeu, 1755, at the capture of Fort Bull by de Lery, 1756, and at Chouaguen (Oswego). Wounded at Niagara, 1759, and taken prisoner. Died at Blois, France. *Oil.*

19. De Montigny, Charlotte Trottier Des Rivieres, born 1723. Daughter of Julien des Rivieres, and wife of the Chevalier J. B. Testard de Montigny. *Oil.*

20. De Montigny, Marie de la Porte Louvigny, daughter of the Governor of Three Rivers and wife of Sieur Jacques Testard de Montigny, born 1696, died 1763. *Oil.*

21. De Montigny, Jacques Testard, born 1663, died 1737. Knight of St. Louis, Captain. One of the greatest warriors of early Canada. " Thirty-five years of active service and forty wounds;—such are the titles which recommend him to posterity," says l'Abbe Daniel. *Oil.* (18 to 21, painted from family miniatures.)

By Subscription.

22. Dupré, Colonel Hypolite Saint-George Le Compte. Captain under the Marquis Duquesne. Commanded the Canadian Militia during the siege of Quebec, 1775-6. In consequence of his behavior during the siege, he was appointed, 4th March, 1778, Commandant of Quebec, by General Sir Guy Carleton. *Oil.*

23. Hocquart, Gilles. Fourth Intendant of New France, from 1731 to 1748. Next to Talon, he was the most active of the Intendants. *Oil.* *Hon. Judge Baby.*

24. D'Amours, Mathieu, Sieur de Clignancour, born 1618, died 1698. Brother of Madame Louis-Theandre Chartier de Lotbiniere. His daughter Marguerite became the wife of Jacques Testard de Montigny. (See 21). *Oil.*

By Subscription.

25. Prevost, General Sir George, born 1767, died 1816. Governor in Chief and Commander of the forces in all British North America, 1811 to 1814. Successfully defended Canada for nearly three years under circumstances of peculiar difficulty. *Oil.*

Hon. Judge Baby.

26. Viger, Jacques. First Mayor of Montreal. A learned Canadian antiquarian, born Montreal, 1787; died 1858. Compiled two valuable works, his *Sabretache*, now in Laval University, Quebec, of twenty volumes in quarto;—the other known as Viger's *Album*. *Oil.*

Hon. Judge Baby.

27. Pothier, Hon. Toussaint, Seigneur of Fief Lagauchetiere. A partner in the old North-West Company. Major in the corps of Voyageurs who took Makinac in the war of 1812; Legislative Councillor 1823; member of the special Council, 1838. A man of great influence in his time. *Oil.* *Wm. Selby, Esq.*

28. Christie, General Gabriel, born 1722, died 1799. Brevet Major under Amherst at the conquest of Canada i

1759. Commander-in-chief in Canada, 1798. (See 128, 129 and de Vaudreuil Room 1 to 5.) *Oil.*

29. Campbell, Col. John, of the Indian Department. Married a daughter of La Corne de St. Luc. *Oil.*
Archbishopric of Montreal.

30. Bourdages, Louis le, Notary, Lieutenant-Colonel of Militia. Canadian patriot during the early years of the 19th century. Sat in the House of Assembly of Lower Canada, for Yamaska and Richelieu, from 1803 until his death in 1833. *Oil.* *Madame Lussier.*

31. Woolryche, James. A prominent merchant in the early years of the last century, painted about 1790. Large proprietor in the Townships. *Oil.*
W. D. Lighthall, Esq., K.C.

32. Selby, William Dunbar, M.D. A practitioner of much repute. Married Melle. Marguerite Baby, September 4th, 1815. Died at Montreal, Feb. 3rd, 1829. *Oil.* (See 4, 27, 13.) *Wm. Selby, Esq.*

33. Hart, Ezekiel. Born 1767, died 1843. Second son of Aaron Hart, the first British merchant who settled at Three Rivers, 1760. Served in the War of 1812. Popular member L. A. *Oil.* *Edgar J. M. Hart, Esq.*

34. The Honorable Judge Baby (Louis-Francois-Georges), descended from Jacques Baby de Ranville, officer in the celebrated Regiment of Carignan-Sallieres, 1663. Born Montreal, 26th August, 1832. Queen's Counsel, 1873. Minister of Inland Revenue. Judge of the Court of Queen's Bench, 1881. Retired 1896. Knight Grand Cross of St. Gregory the Great. One of the founders of the Historical Society, and for more than twenty years President of the Numismatic and Antiquarian Society of Montreal. One of the principal founders of this Museum and Portrait Gallery, and one of the largest contributors to its success. Died May 13th, 1906. *Oil.* (See 12, 13.)

35. Holton, Hon. Luther H. Member of the Executive Council, 1858. M. P. 1867. Was many times President of the Board of Trade, a Harbor Commissioner and Alderman of Montreal. *Crayon.*
Wm. Drysdale, Esq.

36. Dauversiere, J. Leroyer de la. Member of the *Compagnie de Montreal*, its organizer and general agent, and with M. Olier shares in the foundation of Ville-Marie. Died 1660. *Crayon.*

37. Crequi, l'Abbe Jean-Antoine-Aide. Born at Quebec, April 6, 1749. Ordained priest October 24, 1773; died December 7, 1780. The first Canadian painter. Several of his paintings are in the basilica at Quebec. The painting of the " *Annonciation* " over the main altar in the church at l'Islet, is also by him. *Crayon.*

38. Paquin, l'Abbe Jacques, Parish priest at St. Eustache, in 1837. Wrote an account of the insurrection at St. Eustache, 1837-38, much sought after. Also the first ecclesiastical history of Canada, the manuscript of which was unfortunately lost. *Crayon.*

38½. Casgrain, Abbe H. Raymond. Born Riviere Ouelle, 1831; died Quebec, 1904. Famous French-Canadian historian. *Crayon.*   *Hon. Judge Baby.*

39. Beaubien, Dr. Pierre, born 1795, died 1881. Represented Montreal 1841 to 1844, and Chambly 1848 to 1851. Married Justine, daughter of Hon. C. E. Casgrain, Seigneur of Riviere Ouelle. *Crayon.*
    Hon. Louis Beaubien.

40. Meilleur, Jean-Baptiste, born 1796, died 1878. Litterateur. Superintendent of Public Instruction. *Crayon.*

41. Chauveau, Hon. Pierre J. O. Born 1820, died 1890. Eminent French Canadian orator and able writer. Premier of Quebec, 1867 to 1873. Speaker of the Dominion Senate, 1873 to 1874. For many years Superintendent of Education and later Sheriff of Montreal. *Crayon.*

42. Tache, Hon. Sir Etienne-Pascal, aide-de-camp to the Queen, born 1795, died 1865. Lieutenant in the Canadian Voltigeurs, 1812. Speaker of the Legislative Council, 1856, and the head of the administration of the Province. In 1858 the Queen personally conferred the honor of Knighthood upon him. *Crayon.*

43. Tache, J. C., M.D. Born 1821. One of the cleverest men the Province has produced. Represented Rimouski for many years, in Parliament. Was Canadian Commissioner to the Paris Exhibition in 1855. Created Knight of the Legion of Honor by Napoleon III. Wrote many pamphlets and books; author of " *Trois Legendes de mon pays.*" *Crayon.*

44. Dorion, Sir Antoine Aime, born 1818, died 1891. Minister in the Mackenzie Cabinet. Chief Justice of the Court of Queen's Bench, 1874. *Crayon.*

45. Lajoie, Antoine Gérin, born 1824, died 1882. French-Canadian author. Wrote the well-known *Le Canadien Errant*, one of the most popular songs of the French-Canadian people. Editor of *La Minerve* from 1845 to 1852 and later assistant Librarian of the Library of Parliament. *Crayon.*

46. Dunn, Oscar. Brilliant writer. Died 1880. *Crayon.*

47. Provencher, Joseph-Alfred-Norbert, born Jan. 6, 1843, died Oct. 28, 1887. French-Canadian writer. Editor of *La Minerve* and *La Presse*. *Crayon.*

48. Marmette, Joseph, born 1845, died 1895. French-Canadian writer of some repute. Appointed to the Archives Department and sent to Paris to copy historical documents relating to Canada. Author of several works of fiction, *Francois de Bienville, l'Intendant Bigot*, le *Chevalier de Mornac, etc., etc.* Much esteemed. *Crayon.*

48½. Quesnel, Joseph. French-Canadian poet, dramatist and composer. Born France, 1750, died Montreal, 1809. In 1778 he produced "*Colas et Colinette ou le Bailli Dupé*," a comedy in three acts, printed at Quebec, and performed at Montreal in 1790. "*Lucas et Cecile*," a musical operetta; "*Les Republicains Francais*," a comedy. These pieces were extremely popular. *Crayon.*

49. Quesnel, Hon. Frederic Auguste. Talented pleader and member of Parliament. Opposed the Union in 1823 and in 1843 was appointed a member of the Legislative Council. *Crayon.*

50. Bibaud, Michel, born 1782, died 1857. French-Canadian writer of note. Labored hard in defence of Canadian nationality and for the preservation of the French language. Was proprietor of *L'Aurore des Canadas, La Bibliotheque Canadienne, Le Magazine du Bas-Canada, l'Observateur Canadien, Epitres et Satires*, etc., etc. He wrote the first history of Canada in French since the conquest, also an "*Arithmetique Elementaire*" and edited the "*Voyages de Franchere.*" *Crayon.*

51. Margry, Pierre. French author, and eminent geographer, who devoted his attention to the Antiquities of America. Author of volumes regarding the French in North America. *Crayon.*

52. Roebuck, Right Hon. Arthur, born 1801, died 1879. Came to Canada when quite young, was educated here, but returned to England in 1824. Studied law, published several books relating to Canadian matters. In 1832, was elected to House of Commons. Took an active

interest in Canadian affairs. In 1835 the Legislative Assembly of Quebec named him agent of the Province. *Crayon.*

53. Heavysege, Charles. Author of "Saul: a Drama in three parts," 1857. "Count Filippo: or The Unequal Marriage: a Drama in five acts," 1860, "Jepthah's Daughter," 1865, and "The Advocate: a Novel," 1865. *Crayon.*   *W. D. Lighthall, Esq. K.C.*

54. McGee, Hon. Thomas D'Arcy. Born in Ireland, April 13, 1825. Assassinated at Ottawa, April 1868. A patriot, poet, orator and statesman. Was involved in the Irish insurrection of 1848. Went to the United States, and later took up his residence in Canada. In 1857, was elected for the Western division of Montreal, which he continued to represent till his death. One of the Fathers of Confederation. Was accorded a public funeral in Montreal. *Crayon.*

55. De Salaberry, Col. Alphonse Melchior d'Irumberry, son of the hero of Chateauguay. Called to the Legislative Council in 1837, later was appointed Deputy-Adjutant-General of Militia and held that office at the time of his death which occurred in March, 1867, aged 52 years. Married Delle Emilie Guy, a daughter of the Hon. Louis Guy, King's Notary, at Montreal. (See 14.) *Crayon.*

56. General Benjamin Durban, Commander of the Forces in Canada in 1849. Died in Montreal and was buried in the old Military burying ground on Papineau Road. *Engraving.*

The foregoing eighteen Portraits presented by Hon. Judge Baby.

COATS OF ARMS.

57. Montmagny.
   Arms of Sieur Charles Huauit de Montmagny, Governor of Canada, 1636 to 1647.

58. D'Ailleboust de Coulonge, died 1660.
   Arms of Sieur Louis D'Ailleboust de Coulonge, Governor of Canada, 1648 to 1651. Administrator 1657-58.

59. Lauzon.
   Arms of Sieur Jean de Lauson, Governor of Canada, 1651 to 1656.

60. De Mesy.
   Arms of Chevalier Augustin Saffray-Mesy, Governor of Canada, 1663 to 1665. Died at Quebec, 1665.

61. De Tracy.
Arms of Alexander de Prouville, Marquis de Tracy, Viceroy of Canada, 1665.

62. Frontenac.
Arms of Louis de Buade, Count de Palluau et de Frontenac, Governor of Canada. Assumed the government in 1672. Built Fort Frontenac, was recalled in 1682. In 1689, reappointed Governor. In 1690, defeated Sir William Phipps and the English fleet before Quebec. Frontenac was a bold and valorous soldier and a most successful administrator. He died in 1698, and was buried in the Recollet Church at Quebec.

63. De la Barre.
Arms of Sieur le Febvre de la Barre, Governor of Canada, 1682 to 1685.

64. Denonville.
Arms of Jacques Rene de Brisay, Marquis Denonville, Governor of Canada, 1685 to 1689.

65. Raudot.
Arms of Jacques Raudot, Intendant of New France, 1705 to 1712.

66. Louis XIV.
Arms of Louis XIV, King of France.

67. Begon.
Arms of Sieur Michel Begon, Eighth Intendant of New France, 1712 to 1725.

68. Beauharnois.
Arms of Charles, Marquis de Beauharnois, Governor of Canada, 1726 to 1747.

69. Galissoniere.
Arms of Rolland-Michel Barrin, Count de la Galissoniere, Governor of Canada, 1747 to 1749.

70. Jonquiere, died May 17, 1752, aged 67 years.
Arms of Jacques-Pierre de Taffanel, Marquis de la Jonquiere, Governor of Canada, 1749 to 1752.

71. Duquesne.
Arms of the Marquis Duquesne de Menneville, Governor of Canada, 1752 to 1755.

72. Hocquart.
Arms of Sieur Gilles Hocquart, Eleventh Intendant of New France, 1731 to 1748.

73. Talon.
Arms of Jean Talon, Baron d'Orsainville. First Intendant of New France, 1665 to 1672.

74. Cadillac.
Arms of Sieur la Motte-Cadillac, Founder of Detroit 1700.

75. Dorchester.
Arms of Guy Carleton, Lord Dorchester, Governor-General of Canada, 1766 to 1796.

76. Haldimand.
Arms of Sir Frederick Haldimand, Lieutenant Governor of Canada, 1778 to 1784.

(The foregoing Coats-of-Arms were painted by Baron Holmfeldt.) *By Purchase.*

77. 78. Montcalm, Louis-Joseph de Saint Veran, Marquis de, born 1712, died 1759. In 1756 was appointed to command the French troops in Canada. Took Fort Ontario at Oswego, victoriously repulsed the English at Carillon (Ticonderoga), and Fort William Henry at the head of Lake George. Mortally wounded at the battle of the Plains of Abraham, Sept. 13 1759. Interred in the Ursuline Convent, Quebec. *Lithograph.*

Hon. Judge Baby.

79. 80. Wolfe, General James.—*Vide* No. 248.

81. Montgomery, General Richard. A Major-General in the revolutionary army, born in Ireland, 1737. Was with Wolfe at the taking of Quebec. Settled in New York. Commanded the Continental Forces on the invasion of Canada. Fell bravely Dec. 31, 1775, in his attack on Quebec. *Engraving.*

82. Arnold, Benedict. Associated with Montgomery in the attack on Quebec, 1775. Became a traitor to the American cause. Died in London, 1801. *Engraving.*

83. Lymburner, Adam. Highly respected merchant of Quebec, in 1775. Member of the Executive Council. Called to the Bar of the House of Commons to give evidence regarding Canadian affairs, where he strongly opposed the separation of the two provinces. He died at his residence, Russel Square, London, Jan. 10, 1836. *Engraving.* *Alfred Sandham, Esq.*

84. Yonge, Sir George, Right Hon., Secretary of War, 1791. Yonge Street, Toronto, is named after him. A personal friend of Governor Simcoe. *Engraving.*

R. B. Angus, Esq.

85. General Dumas, who succeeded to the command of Fort Duquesne, after de Beaujeu. From a family painting. *Photo.*

86. Carroll, Charles of Carrollton. One of the signers of the Declaration of Independence, accompanied Benj. Franklin and Samuel Chase to Montreal, in 1776, as one of the three envoys sent by Congress. Was a guest in the Chateau while here. Died Nov. 4, 1832, almost a century old, the sole survivor of the signers of the Declaration of Independence. *Engraving.*
Hon. Judge Baby.

87. Brock, Sir Isaac. This renowned general was born in the Island of Guernsey on Oct. 6, 1769. Colonel of the 49th Regiment. In 1811, promoted to the rank of Major-General, fell victorious at the battle of Queenston Heights, Oct. 13, 1812. *Lithograph.*
Dr. W. G. Nicholl.

88. Mackenzie, Sir Alexander. In 1789, explored the coun ry between the Pacific and Hudson Bay, and discovered the great river which bears his name. One of the founders of the celebrated North-West Company. *Photo.* *Dr. Mackenzie Forbes.*

89. Selby, Miss Dunbar, wife of Dr. George Selby. Pastel.

90. Selby, George, M.D., born 1760, died 1835. Born in England and educated at the College of St. Omer, in France. Came to Canada at the age of 21 years, married Miss Dunbar, daughter of Major Dunbar and Melle. Josephte Catherine Fleury Deschambault. *Pastel.*
Wm. Selby, Esq.

91. Ferland, l'Abbé, J. B. A., born 1805, died 1865. Distinguished French-Canadian author. Wrote History of Canada, and several other works. *Lithograph.*
Hon. Judge Baby.

92. Laval, Francois de Montmorency de, born 1622, died 1708. First Roman Catholic Bishop of Canada. Arrived in Quebec, 1659, founded the Quebec Seminary, 1663. To his high descent, he owed much of the influence which he exer. 1 in the Civil, as well as the ecclesiastical affairs of the ' ony. *Lithograph.*
R. W. McLachlan, Esq.

93. De Gaspé, Philippe Aubert, born 1786, died 1871. Canadian *litterateur.* Sheriff of Quebec. Author (being then over eighty years of age), of " *Les Anciens Canadiens,*" and " *Memoires,*" in which he well portrayed the character and manners of the old French-Canadians. *Lithograph.* *Alfred Aubert de Gaspé, Esq.*

94. St. Martin, Nicholas. A distinguished Montreal merchant. *Photo.*

95. General de Levis. *Vide* No. 6.
96. De Malartic, Anne-Joseph-Hippolite, Comte de Maures. Born in 1730, died in 1800. A distinguished officer. Highly esteemed by General Montcalm. Upon returning to France, he became a Lieutenant-General, and Governor of the Isle of France. *Photo.*
97. La Perouse, Jean-Francois Galoup de. Distinguished French navigator. Born 1741. Served in aid of the Americans 1775, at Hudson's Bay. Sent by the French Government on a voyage of discovery (1785), to the South Seas and Pacific Ocean, where he visited many islands, etc. In March, 1791, he left Botany Bay and was never afterwards heard of. *Photo.*   *Hon. Judge Baby.*
98. De Levis. Marquis et Marquise. Photographs of two oil portraits in possession of Wm. Gilley, Esq., Birmingham, Eng. Tradition asserts them to be Montcalm and wife, but possibly Levis and wife.
    W. D. Lighthall, Esq., K.C.
99. Salaberry, de, Vice-Admiral of France under Henry IV. *Photo.* (See 14, 55, 100).
    W. D. Lighthall, Esq., K.C.
100. Salaberry, Michel d'Irumberry de, died 1772. The first of the name who came to Canada. Arrived at Quebec in 1735, on the "*Anglesea*," frigate. Grand-father of the hero of Chateauguay. Married 1st, Delle Rouer de Villeray; 2nd, Delle Madeleine Louise Duchesnay. *Photo* (See 14, 55, 99.)   *W. D. Lighthall, Esq., K.C.*
101. Tanguay, Monsignor Cyprien. Born Quebec, 1819; priest 1843. In 1865, Author of "*Le Dictionnaire Genealogique des Familles Canadiennes*" "*Le Repertoire du Clerge*," "*A Travers les Registres*," etc., etc. A man of high culture, deeply versed in Canadian history. Died Ottawa, April, 1902. *Photo.*   *Hon. Judge Baby.*
102. Haliburton, Judge Thomas Chandler, a native of Nova Scotia, author of *Sam Slick*, the *Bubbles of Canada*, the *Clockmaker*, etc., etc. The father of American humor. *Woodcut.*
103. Cunard, Sir Samuel, the founder of the Cunard Line of Steamships, the first regular line between Europe and America. *Woodcut.*   *H. J. Tiffin, Esq.*
104. The three first Governors of the Honorable the Hudson's Bay Company:—
    1. H.R.H. Prince Rupert, a distinguished name in the the history of Charles I., born 1619. Remarkable for his impetuous gallantry and chivalrous bearing, died 1682.

2. H.R.H. James, Duke of York, afterwards James II.
3. Lord Churchill Duke of Marlborough. *Photo.*

Chs. T. Hart, Esq.

105. Nansen, Fridjof. The celebrated Arctic Explorer. *Litho.*

T. O'Leary, Esq.

106. Colbert, Jean Baptiste, Marquis de Segnelai, one of the greatest statesmen of France. Born Paris, 1619, died 1683. Did considerable for the advancement of Canada. *Engraving.*

107. Porteous, Thomas. Montreal merchant. Built the first water works in Montreal, 1801, and the bridges at Repentigny in 1808. *Silhouette.*

Thos. Porteous, Esq.

108. Poulin, Etienne. Veteran of 1812, was at Lundy's Lane and Chrysler's Farm. *Lithograph.*

L. A. Poulin, Esq.

109. Isaacson, Robert Philip, popularly known as "Dolly," proprietor of Dolly's Chop House. *Oil.*

J. H. Isaacson, Esq.

110. Dorchester, Guy Carleton, Lord. Born 1725, died 1808. Was with Wolfe at the battle of the Plains of Abraham and with Murray at St. Foye. Governor General of Canada 1767 to 1777 and 1786 to 1796. *Oil.*

By Subscription.

111. Gosford, Earl of, G.C.B. Governor-General from August 1835, to February 26, 1838. Died in England, March 29, 1849. *Oil.*

112. Haldimand, Sir Frederick, K.B., a native of Switzerland, entered the British Army in 1754. Greatly distinguished himself at the battles of Ticonderoga and Oswego. Lieutenant-Governor of Canada, June 27, 1778, to Nov. 18, 1784. Died in England. *Oil.*

By Subscription.

113. Metcalfe, Charles Theophilus, Baron Metcalfe, K.G., C.B. Born 1785, died 1846. A distinguished British Statesman, Governor of Jamaica, 1842, and Governor-General of Canada, 1843 to 1845. *Oil.*

W. B. Mathewson, Esq.

114. Sydenham, Charles Poulett Thompson, created Baron Sydenham and Toronto in 1840. Born 1793, died 1841 Governor-General of Canada 1839 to the time of his death which resulted from an accident while riding near Kingston, Canada. *Oil.* *Wm Kinloch, Esq.*

115. Murray, General, The Hon. James, Lieutenant of Wolfe. First Governor-General of the Province of Quebec, 1763 to 1767. Died in 1794. *Lithograph.*
Hon. Judge Baby.
116. Amherst, General Sir Jeffrey, born 1717, died 1797. Commander-in-Chief of the British Army at the Conquest. Created Baron Amherst, 1787. Received the surrender of Montreal, Sept. 8, 1760. Seat " Montreal," Sevenoaks, Kent, England. *Engraving.*
117. Dalhousie, General George, Earl of. Born 1770, died 1838. Was Governor-General of Canada, 1820 to 1828. A General in the Army and Colonel of 26th Regiment of Foot, saw much active service during the Peninsular War. *Engraving.* *R. B. Angus, Esq.*
118. Colborne, Sir John. Lord Seaton, born 1778, died 1863. In 1829 Lieutenant-Governor of Upper Canada. Commander-in-Chief of Canada, and temporarily Governor-General. Overcame the rebellion of 1837-1838. *Engraving.*
Presented by his son-in-law, General Montgomery Moore.
119. Dufferin, Frederick Temple Blackwood, Earl of, born June 26, 1826. Governor-General, 1872 to 1878. Viceroy of India. *Lithograph.* *Presented by Himself.*
120. Aberdeen, John Charles Hamilton Gordon, Earl of, Aberdeen. Governor-General 1893 to 1898. *Crayon.*
Presented by Himself.
121. Head, Sir Edmund Walker, born 1805. Governor-General 1855 to 1861. *Crayon.*
122. Williams of Kars. General Sir William Fenwick, born Annapolis, N.S., 1801; died London, 1883. During the Crimean War made brave defence of Kars. In 1865, was Lieut.-Governor of Nova Scotia; 1870-77 Governor of Gibraltar. *Lithograph.*
123. Richmond, Charles Lennox, fourth Duke of. Born 1764, died 1820, Governor-General of Canada 1819 to August 27, 1820. Died from the bite of a tame fox at a small village on the Ottawa. *Engraving.*
124. Durham, The Earl of. Born 1792, died 1840. Governor-General. Appointed to report on the rebellion of 1837. His acts were marked by liberality and disinterestedness; the minor offenders were pardoned, and eighty of the ringleaders were banished to Bermuda. His famous report resulted in Responsible Government. *Engraving.*
125. Bagot, Sir Charles, G.C.B., born 1781, died 1844. Governor-General, 1842. *Engraving.*
The five foregoing presented by the Hon. Judge Baby.

126. Metcalfe, Lord. *Vide* No. 113.
127. Elgin, Right Hon. Earl of. Born 1811, died 1863. Governor-General of Canada from 1847 to 1854 One of the best known of Canadian Governors. *Oil.*
By Purchase.
128. Burton, General Napier Christie, born 1758, died 1835. Succeeded his father, General Gabriel Christie as Commander-in-Chief of the forces in Canada, 1799. Son-in-law to General Ralph Burton, whose name he assumed. (See 28.) *Oil.*
129. Christie, Mrs. Napier, mother of General Gabriel Christie. (See 28.) *Oil.*
130. De Longueuil, Charles-Colmore Grant, 7th Baron. Born in Montreal 1844, died in New York 1899. *Photograph.*
Baroness de Longueuil.
131. Head, Sir Francis Bond, born 1793, died 1875. Lieutnant-Governor of Upper Canada from 1836 to 1838. Author of an account of the Rebellion in Upper Canada, 1837-38. *Engraving.* *Hon. Judge Baby.*
132. Berthelet, Dame Caroline, wife of the late R. S. M. Bouchette, Commissioner of Customs, painted by himself.
133. Tonnancour, Louise Carrerot, wife of Louis-Joseph-Godfrey de. She belonged to an Acadian family in the King's service. *Madame de Tonnancour.*
134. Mountain, Captain, son of Bishop Mountain, of Quebec, painted by his sister. *Oil.*
W. D. Lighthall, Esq., K.C.
135. Blair, Colonel, a relative of the Selby family. Served in in Canada as Lieutenant in the 93rd Highlanders. *Oil.*
Wm. Selby, Esq.
136. Lennox, Col., son of Lord Lennox. Married Miss Marie-Marguerite de Chapt de La Corne St. Luc, who, upon his death, married Jacques Viger, the distinguished Antiquarian. *Pastel.* (See 4, 5, 29.)
137. Elgin, Right Hon. Earl of. *Vide* No. 127.
138. De Boishébert, Charles de Champ, Governor of Acadia, Allied to the DeRamezay family *Photograph.*
Hon. Judge Baby.
139. De Montmorency, Henri, Duke. Viceroy of Canada, 1620. *Engraving.* *Alfred Sandham, Esq.*
140. Henry de Bourbon, Prince de Condé, Comte de Soissons, Viceroy of Canada, 1612. *Engraving.*
Hon. Judge Baby.

141. Saunders, Admiral Sir Charles, died 1775. Associated with Wolfe, in the siege of Quebec, as the Commander of the fleet. *Engraving.*
W. D. Lighthall, Esq., K.C.

142. Members of the International Commission, Quebec 1898. *Photo.*

143. Group of the Premiers of the British Colonies, London, 1897 at Queen Victoria's Jubilee. *Photo.*
H. J. Tiffin, Esq.

144. Cornwallis, Charles, Marquis, born 1738, died 1800. Major-General in the British Army. Served under Howe and Clinton, surrendered army at Yorktown, after gallant defence, October 19, 1781. *Engraving.*
Hon. Judge Baby.

145. Ouimet, Hon. Gedeon, Prime Minister of Quebec, and later Superintendent of Public Instruction, 1875 to 1895. *Photo.*
Dr. Gustave Ouimet.

146. Isaac Todd, a member of the Old Nor-West Company. *Presented by C. de Lery Macdonald and W. D. Lighthall, Esqs. Oil.*

147. Johnson, Sir John, Major-General, born 1770, died 1830. The only son of Sir William Johnson, of the Mohawk Valley. *Engraving.*
Hon. Judge Baby.

148. Lord Ashburton, John Dunning, an eminent lawyer, born 1731. His grandson figures in the "Ashburton Treaty." *Engraving.*
Chs. T. Hart, Esq.

149. Queen Victoria at the age of nineteen. *Photo.*
H. J. Tiffin, Esq.

150. H. R. H. George Augustus, Prince of Wales, eldest son of George III. *Engraving.*

151. Plan of the City of Quebec, and the Battle of the Plains of Abraham, 1759.
Hon. Judge Baby.

152. Poitras, Alphonse. Gifted French-Canadian writer. *Oil.*
Judge L. W. Sicotte.

153. Gugy, Hon. Louis. Colonel in the War of 1812, and eventually Sheriff of Montreal. *Oil.*
Louis Sutherland, Esq.

154. Lartigue, Jean-Jacques, first R. C. Bishop of Montreal, born 1777, died 1840. *Oil.*

155. Marquette, Jacques, born 1637, died May 18, 1675. Jesuit missionary. With Louis Joliet he discovered the Mississippi, June 17, 1673. *Oil.*

156. Casot, Jean Joseph. Last of the Jesuits who were in Canada at the time of the Conquest. Born October 4, 1728; died at the Jesuits' College, Quebec, March 16, 1800. *Oil.*

157. Le Jeune, Father Paul. Father of the Jesuit Missions in Canada. In 1635, preached the funeral oration over Champlain. Returned to France in 1649. *Oil.*

158. Brebeuf, Father Jean de, of the Society of Jesus, born 1539, died 1649. The most illustrious of the martyrs of New France. Came to Canada in 1646, went on the Huron Mission, fell into the hands of the Iroquois and was cruelly tortured by them. The skull of this martyr is in the Hotel-Dieu Hospital, Quebec. *Oil.*

159. Lalement, Father Gabriel, Jesuit missionary, born 1610, died 1649. Underwent, with Father Brebeuf, the most cruel tortures of martyrdom. *Oil.*

160. Jogues, Father Isaac, born 1598, died 1646. First apostle of the Iroquois. Horribly mutilated by them 1642, delivered by the Dutch and landed in France, returned to Canada, massacred 1646. *Oil.*

161. Lafitau, Father Joseph-Francois de. A celebrated Jesuit missionary among the native tribes of Canada from 1700 to 1717. Discovered the Gin-Seng root in New France. Died in 1740. *Oil.*

162. Charlevoix, Father Pierre-Francois-Xavier, born 1684, died 1761. Celebrated Jesuit writer, for several years a resident in Canada. Author of *"Histoire Generale de la Nouvelle France,"* etc. Was a guest in the Chateau in 1722. *Oil.*

163. Duplessis, Father Francois-Xavier, Jesuit missionary, born in Quebec, 1663; died in Paris. A celebrated pulpit orator. *Oil.*

164. Gamelin, Ignace, born 1698. Married Marie-Louise Dufrost de la Jemerais, 1731, sister of Madame d'Youville. *Oil.* (See 10, 165, 166, 167, 168.)

165. Marie-Louise Dufrost de la Jemerais, sister of Madame d'Youville, and wife of Ignace Gamelin, born 1705; died 1789. *Oil.* (See 164.)

166. Gamelin, Medard, son of Ignace Gamelin and nephew of Madame d'Youville, Lieutenant and Major. Born 1733, died 1778. *Oil.* (See 164.)

167 Porlier, Claude-Cyprien-Jacques, Royal Notary at Montreal. Born 1683, died 1744. *Oil.* (See 164).

168. Cuillerier, Angelique, wife of Claude-Cyprien-Jacques Porlier. Born 1698, died 1781. *Oil.* (See 164.)

No. 154 to No. 168 acquired by Subscription.

169. Panet, Amelie, wife of William Beresy, jr., co-seigneur of d'Ailleboust, daughter of Hon. Judge Pierre-Louis Panet. Died in 1862, at d'Ailleboust. A remarkable woman, by the powers of her intellect and acquirements. *Crayon.*

170. Leprohon, Jean, Madame, nee Mullins. Canadian authoress, born in Montreal, 1832; died 1879. Her first novel, *Ida Beresford*, appeared in 1848. Several of her romances were translated into French. *Crayon.*
Hon. Judge Baby.

171. Louis XV, King of France, when a youth. *Oil.*

172. Soulanges, Chevalier Pierre-Jacques Joybert de, son of Pierre, the Seigneur of Soulanges ,and brother-in-law of Marquis de Vaudreuil, born 1677, died 1703. *Crayon.*

173. Lery, Francois-Joseph Chaussegros de, celebrated engineer under Napoleon. Born Quebec 1754, died France, 1824. His portrait is in the *Invalides* and his name is on the *Arc de Triomphe*, Paris. *Crayon.*

174. St. Ours, Quinson de, Chevalier de St. Louis, officer in the French troops, after the Conquest served in the English army, later again took service in France. Married a Miss Saveuse de Beaujeu. *Crayon.*

175. George III., King of England. *Oil.*
James Coristine, Esq.

176. Cartier, Jacques, died 1554. Discoverer of Canada, 1534. On his second voyage, 1535, he discovered Stadacona (Quebec), and Hochelaga (Montreal). *Oil.*
Richelieu Navigation Co.

177. Lacombe, Patrice. Litterateur, died 1863. *Crayon.*

178. De Boucherville, George Boucher. Litterateur, born 1814. In 1837, was one of the Sons of Liberty. His principal work is "*Une de Perdue et deux de Retrouvees.*" *Crayon.*

179. Cauchon, Hon. Joseph. Born at Quebec Dec., 18 Regarded as one of the first journalists of the Provin. First President of the Senate after Confederation. Lieutenant-Governor of Manitoba 1877; died 1885. *Crayon.*

180. De Courcey, Charles, Litterateur, known by the name of La Roche-Heron. Wrote "*Histoire Ecclesiastique des Etats-Unis*," "*Les Servantes de Dieu en Canada*," etc. *Crayon.*

181. Girouard, Jean-Jacques. Imprisoned during the troubles of 1837. *Crayon.*

182. Viger, Hon. Denis-Benjamin, born 1774, died 1861. Prominent in the controversy which led to the insurrection of 1837-38. Imprisoned 1837. Legislative Councillor 1848. *Crayon.*
Nos. 177 to 182 *presented by the Hon. Judge Baby.*

183. Craig, Sir James, H.K.C.B., born 1750, died 1812. Governor-General of Canada, 1807 to 1811. The whole time of his administration, or nearly all of it, was occupied in rather bitter party bickerings. *Engraving.*
R. B. Angus, Esq.

184. Oronhyatekha, M.D. ("Burning Cloud.") Mohawk Indian Chief, born 1841. Founder of the Independent Order of Foresters. Died 1907. *Photo.*
Victor Morin, Esq.

185. McCully, Hon. Jonathan, one of the founders of Confederation. *Crayon.* *Mrs. Clarence W. McCully.*

186. Fulford, Right Rev. Francis, Metropolitan Bishop of Canada, born 1803; died 1868. *Lithograph.*

187. De Winton, Major-General Sir Francis Walter, G.C. M.G., C.B. Aide-de-camp to General Sir Fenwick Williams, and the Marquis of Lorne. *Lithograph.*
Hon. Judge Baby.

188. Wright, Alonzo. Born at Hull, Que., February 26, 1825. Grandson of Philemen Wright, founder of Hull. *Lithograph.* *P. B. Casgrain, Esq.*

189. McGill, Peter, Hon. Born 1809, died 1860. A prominent Montreal merchant, member of the Legislative Council. President of the Bank of Montreal, etc. Mayor of Montreal from 1840 to 1842. *Engraving.*
Hon. Judge Baby.

190. Members of the Seigniorial Tenure Court, Quebec, 1855. *Lithograph.* *W. D. Cruikshank, Esq.*

191. Mountain, Right Rev. G. J., Lord Bishop of Quebec born 1789, Son of the first Anglican Bishop of Quebec Ordained in 1813; consecrated Bishop of Montreal, 1836 *Lithograph.*

192. Baldwin, Rt. Rev. Maurice S., Bishop of Huron. Born 1836. Ordained 1861. Dean of Montreal, 1879, Bishop of Huron, 1883. Died 1904. *Lithograph.*

193. Francis I., King of France and first King of Canada. Born 1494, died 1547. Under Francis I. Jacques-Cartier discovered Canada. *Engraving.*
Alfred Sandham, Esq.

194. Mercier, Hon. Honore, Premier of Quebec. *Oil.*
Dr. P. E. Mount.

195. D'Argenson, Pierre de Voyer, Viscount. Born 162 died 1709. Succeeded de Lauson as Governor of Ne France, in 1658. *Engraving.*

196. Begon, Michel, Chevalier, Seigneur de la Picardiere, etc tenth Intendant of New France, 1712-1726. *Engravi*

197. D'Iberville, Le Moyne. *Vide No.* 3.

198. Galissoniere, Roland-Michel Barrin, Count de l Administrator New France 1747 to 1749, during tl imprisonment in England of Admiral de la Jonquier the Governor. He was a distinguished marine officer *savant* and *litterateur*; died 1756. *Engraving.*
Hon. Judge Baby.

199. Bougainville, Louis Antoine, born 1729, died 1811 Distinguished for his maritime discoveries. Serve under Montcalm. *Engraving.*

200. Papineau, Hon. Louis Joseph, born 1789, died 1875 Captain of militia during the war of 1812. In 181 Speaker of the Lower Canada Assembly. Inspired th insurrection of 1837. Exiled eight years. *Lithograph*
Hon. Judge Baby.

201. Fabre, Edouard, born 1799, died 1854. Took part in the insurrection of 1837-38 and was imprisoned. Father of the late Archbishop of Montreal. *Lithograph.*
J. B. Doutre, Esq.

202. Lafontaine, Sir L.-H., Bart., born 1807, died 1864. Celebrated statesman, antiquarian and lawyer. Implicated in the insurrection of 1837, went to France, returned and became leader of his party. Chief-Justice of the Court of Queen's Bench, 1853. *Oil.*
By Purchase.

203. Morin, Hon. Auguste-Norbert, born 1803. Speaker of the House 1848-51. *Lithograph.*
Hon. Judge Baby.

204. Letellier de St. Just, Hon. Luc, born 1820, died 1881. Third Lieutenant-Governor of the Province of Quebec, from 1876 to 1879. *Lithograph.*
P. B. Casgrain, Esq.

205. Sir Alured Clarke. Lieutenant-Governor from 1792 to 1793. Governor-General of India and Field Marshal. Died 1832. *Photo.* *Chs. T. Hart, Esq.*

206. Lord Aylmer. The Right Honorable Matthew Whitworth, born 1775. Fought in Spain at Talavera, Buasco, Fuentes d'Oner, Vittoria, the siege of Bayonne, etc., etc. In 1828, Governor-General of Canada. Died in London, 1860. *Photo.*   *Chs. T. Hart, Esq.*

207. Sir James Kempt, born 1765. Served all through the Peninsular War, and commanded a brigade at Waterloo. Governor-General 1828 to 1830. Died 1855. *Photo.*
Chs. T. Hart, Esq.

208. Maitland, Sir Peregrine, G.C.B., born 1777, died 1854. Lieutenant-Governor of Upper Canada. Crayon.
Hon. Judge Baby.

209. H.R.H. the Prince of Wales, at Rosemount, Aug., 1860. The Duke of Newcastle, Sir Edmund Walker Head, Governor-General, Lt.-Col. Teesdale and Col. Bruce. *Photo.*   *Chs. T. Hart, Esq.*

210. Garneau, Francois-Xavier, born 1809; died 1866. The Emminent French Canadian Historian. *Photo.*
Hon. Judge Baby.

211. Joliette, The Honorable Berthelemy; born 1789, died 1850. Founder of Joliette. A statue was erected to him at Joliette, 1902. *Engraving.*
Hon. Judge Baby.

212. Mackenzie, William Lyon, born 1795, died 1861. First Mayor of Toronto, 1836. Prominent in the Insurrection of 1837-38. *Engraving.*   *A. Sandham, Esq.*

213. Moquin, Louis, born 1787, died 1825. An able French-Canadian jurisconsult. *Photo.*

214. Cross, Judge A., Judge of the Court of Queen's Bench Montreal. *Engraving.*

215. Peel, the Right Hon. Sir Robert. Eminent British Statesman. *Engraving.*
The above three presented by Hon. Judge Baby.

216. Boscawen, Admiral Edward. Naval commander, born 1711, died 1761. In 1758, in conjunction with Lord Amherst, captured Louisburg. *Engraving.*
H. H. Lyman, Esq.

217. Franklin, Benjamin, born 1706, died 1790. Was a guest in this Chateau in 1776, together with Samuel Chase and Charles Carroll, of Carrollton, Commissioners sent the Canadian people by the United States Congress. *Engraving.*   *Hon. Judge Baby.*

218. Gates, General Horatio. Born 1728, died 1806. Maj͏̈ General in the American Army, during the War Independence. Defeated Bourgoyne, October 8, 177͏̈ *Engraving.*   *Hon. Judge Baby.*

219. Sherbrooke, Sir John Cope, Governor-General of Canad͏̈ from 1816 to 1818, on account of ill-health he requeste͏̈ his recall. *Engraving.*   *Chs. T. Hart, Esq.*

220. Lisgar, Lord (Sir John Young), Governor-General ͏̈ Canada from 1869 to 1872. *Engraving.*
            Alfred Sandham, Esq.

221. D'Urban, General. *Vide No.* 56.

222. Durnford, Lt.-General Elias Walker, born July 30. 1774͏̈ died 1850. Commanded the Royal Engineers in Canad͏̈ 1820-31; superintended the erection of Fort Lennox an͏̈ of the Citadel at Quebec. Grandfather of the dono͏̈ *Photo.*   *George Durnford, Esq.*

223. Provencher, Mgr. Joseph-Norbert, First R. C. Bishop ͏̈ the North-West. Born at Nicolet, February 12, 1787͏̈ Died 1853. *Photo.* *Mrs. J. A. N. Provencher.*

224. Parent, Etienne, born 1801, died 1874. Talente͏̈ French-Canadian writer and journalist. Father-in-la͏̈ of Gerin-Lajoie, the noted librarian and writer (die͏̈ 1872); Evariste Gelinas, the well-known chronicler (die͏̈ 1882), and Benjamin Sulte, the historian. *Engrav͏̈ ιg.*
            B. Sulte, Esq.

225. McGill, Hon. James; born 1744, died 1813. Born i͏̈ Scotland, came to Montreal at an early age and engage͏̈ successfully in mercantile pursuits; member of th͏̈ Executive Council, 1793; was a Colonel and Brigadier͏̈ General during the War of 1812. Founder of McGi͏̈ University. He married on December 2, 1776, Charlott͏̈ Guillemin, widow of the late Francois Amable Trottie͏̈ Des Rivieres, a daughter of the late Guillaume Guillemin͏̈ in his lifetime Councillor of the King of France ͏̈ Canada, Lieutenant-General of the Admiralty of Quebec͏̈ and Judge of the Court of Prerogatives.

226. Workman, William, Mayor of Montreal, 1868 to 1870.

227. Caron, the Hon. Rene-Edouard, Lieutenant-Governor o͏̈ the Province of Quebec, from 1873 to 1876. Born 1800͏̈ died 1876. Was the first Mayor of Quebec. *Engraving*

228. Masson, Hon. Louis R., born 1833. Minister of Militi͏̈ and Defence, 1878. Lieutenant-Governor of the Prov͏̈ ince of Quebec, 1884, died 1903. *Photo.*

229. Angers, Hon. Auguste Real Born 1838. Lieutenant-Governor of Quebec 1887. *Photo.*
230. Chapleau, Hon Jos. A. *Vide No.* 250.
231. Macdonald, the Right Hon. Sir John Alexander, K.B., and K.G.C.M.G. Born January 11, 1815, died June 6, 1891. Great Canadian statesman. Premier 1867 to 1873, and again from 1878 to the time of his death in 1891. One of the Fathers of Confederation. *Photo.*
232. Abbott, Hon. John Joseph Caldwell, D.C.L. Born 1821, died 1893. Leader of the Senate 1887, until June, 1891, when he became Premier. Died 1892. *Photo.*
233. Thompson, Sir John. Born 1844, died 1894. Premier of the Dominion at the time of his death, which happened suddenly at Windsor Castle when on a visit to the Queen. *Photo.*
234. Mowat, Hon. Oliver. Born in Kingston, July 22, 1820. Premier of Ontario, 1872-1896. Minister o Justice, 1896. Lieut.-Governor of Ontario, Nov., 1897, died 1903. *Photo.*
235. Tilley, Sir Samu'i Leonard, K.C.M.G. and C.B. Born 1818. Minister ,; Customs 1867 to 1873. Lieutenant-Governor of New Brunswick, 1873. Died 1896. *Photo.*

225 to 235 prese ted by the Hon. Judge Baby.

236. Cartier, Sir George-Etienne. Born 1814, died in London, 1873. Provincial Secretary 1856, leader of the Lower Canada section of the Government in 1857, and Premier in 1858. Was on of the principal authors of Confederation. His remains were brought to Canada and accorded a public funeral. *Oil.*

Presented to the Chateau by his daughter, Miss Cartier, Paris.

237. Howe, Hon. Joseph. Born 1804. Son of an U.E. Loyalist. One of the earliest advocates of British American Union. Orator, *litterateur*, journalist, politician, statesman and diplomat; genial and witty. Lieutenant-Governor of Nova Scotia, 1873, and died June 1, same year. *Lithograph. J. J. Stewart, Esq.*
238. Mackenzie, Hon. Alexander. Born 1822. Leader of Ontario Reform Opposition, in the House of Commons, from 1867 to 1873, when elected leader of the whole Oppostiion party. Prime Minister, 1873. Died 1892. *Lithograph.* *Hon Judge Baby.*
239. Nelson, Wolfred, M.D. Born 1792. Membe of Parliament for Sorel in 1827. Commanded the insurgents at St. Denis, Nov. 23, 1837. Exiled to Bermuda, 1838

to 1842. Re-elected to Parliament by the County of Richelieu from 1844 to 1848. Was twice Mayor of Montreal. *Lithograph.*   *J. B. Doutre, Esq.*

240. Viger, Hon. D. B. *Vide No.* 182.

241½. Carroll, Rev. John, Cousin of Carroll of Carrollton, whom he accompanied to Montreal in 1776. First Roman Catholic Bishop of Baltimore. Died 1815. *Engraving.*   *Hon. Judge Baby.*

242. Commission for the Codification of the Laws of Lower Canada
   Hon. D. C. Day, Hon. R. E. Caron and Hon. A. N. Morin, Commissioners. J. U. Beaudry and T. McCord, Secretaries.   *Hon. Judge Baby.*

243. Bouchette, Joseph. Born 1774, died 1841. Canada's ablest topographer, Surveyor-General of Lower Canada. A protege of H.R.H. the Duke of Kent. He made many valuable plans of Canada, and published his valuable "Topography of Lower Canada," in 1815. *Oil.*
   J. E. M. Whitney, Esq.

244. Gates, Hon. Horatio. Leading Montreal merchant. Third President of the Bank of Montreal. Portrait painted by A. Parke, in 1818. *Oil.*
   Hodgson, Sumner & Co.

245. Members of the first Parliament of the Province of Ontario, 1870.   *J. Wolferstan Thomas, Esq.*

246. Rogers, Robert Major, of Rogers' Rangers. Was with Amherst at the capitulation of Montreal, 1760, and fought throughout the Revolutionary War. *Photo.*
   Lt.-Col. H. C. Rogers.

247. Rageneau, Father Paul, Jesuit Missionary. He it was who, in 1650, conducted the miserable remnant of the Huron nation to Quebec. Returned to France in 1666 and died at Paris, 1680, aged 75. *Oil.*
   By Subscription.

248. Wolfe, General James. Born 1726, died 1759. Commanded against Quebec in 1759. Succeeded in carrying his forces up the cliff to the Plains of Abraham and compelled Montcalm to fight. The battle was strenuously contested, but the French at length gave way. Wolfe and Montcalm were mortally wounded, September 13, 1759. *Oil.*   *James Morgan, Esq.*

249. Labrie, Jacques, M.B. Born 1783, died 1831. A zealous French-Canadian patriot. Did a great deal for the spread of education. Established and edited the

Courrier de Quebec, in 1807. Wrote one of the first histories of Canada, but died before he was able to have it published, and ultimately it was destroyed by fire at St. Benoit during the troubles of 1837. *Photo.*

250. Chapleau, Hon. Jos.-Adolphe. Born 1840, died 1898. Lieut.-Governor of Quebec 1892 to 1898. *Lithograph.*
Hon. Judge Baby.

251. De Lotbiniere, Michel Chartier, Marquis. Born 1728, died 1798. Chevalier de St. Louis. Engineer in Chief of New France, Seigneur of Lotbiniere, Vaudreuil, Rigaud. Built the forts of Carillon and Isle aux Noix. It was upon his advice that Montcalm attacked Fort William Henry 1757, and waited for Abercrombie at Ticonderoga 1758. Allied to the Vaudreuil family. *Oil.*
Hon. Judge Baby and W. D. Lighthall, Esq., K.C.

252. De Vaudreuil, Philippe de Rigaud, Marquis, Born 1643, died 10th October, 1725. A Lieutenant-General in the French army, and Governor-General of New France from 1703 to 1725. Married Louise E. Joybert, daughter of Chevalier Joybert de Soulanges. *Oil.*
Hon. Judge Baby and W. D. Lighthall, Esq., K.C.

253. De Vaudreuil Cavagnal, Pierre de Rigaud, Marquis. Born at Quebec 1698, died in France 1764, was son of the preceding, the last Governor of Canada under French domination. In 1733 he was appointed Governor of Three Rivers, in 1743, of Louisiana and in 1755, Governor-General of New France. Signed the capitulation of Montreal, 8th Sep , 1760. *Oil.*
Hon. Judge Baby and W. D. Lighthall, Esq., K.C.

254. De Vaudreuil, Francois-Pierre de Rigaud, Chevalier. Born 1703, died in France later than 1770. Brother of the last Governor. Was Lieutenant-Governor of Quebec in 1748, Governor of Three Rivers 1749, and was appointed Governor of Montreal 1757. Married to Louise-Therese Fleury de La Gorgendiere. *Oil.*
Hon. Judge Baby and W. D. Lighthall, Esq., K.C.

255. Baldwin, Hon. Robert, C.B. Born 1804. In September of 1842 became Attorney-General for Upper Canada, Mr. Lafontaine occupying the corresponding office in Lower Canada and dividing with him the dual premiership. Taking again the same office in 1848, he held it till July 1851. Died 1858. *Oil.*   *By Purchase.*

256. Brown, Hon. George. Prominent Canadian statesman. One of the "Fathers of Confederation." Born 1818, died 1880. *Lithograph.*   *Dr. W. G. Nicholl.*

257, 258. Thomas Walker and wife. Prominent magistra and merchant in 1775. Entertained Benjamin Frankli Carroll and Chase, the envoys of the Continent Congress. *Oil.*   *W. D. Lighthall, Esq., K.C.*

259. Members of the Montreal Snowshoe Club in 1875. Th Earl of Dufferin in the group. *Photo.*
                                         Dr. W. G. Nicholl.

260. A contemporary portrait of George II., of England from the collection of M. Lajeunesse, father of Mde. Albani. *Oil.*   *W. D. Lighthall, Esq., K.C.*

261. Portrait of Frs. Corbin, aged 63 years. Drawn at Sorel, 7th April, 1797, by Dulongpre. *Pastel.*

262. Portrait of Mde. Frs. Corbin at the age of 48 years. Drawn by Dulongpre, at Sorel, 7th April, 1797. *Pastel.*
                                         Mde. Lusignan.

263. Portrait of Matthew Lymburner, a prominent merchant of Quebec in 1775. Brother of Adam Lymburner for which see No. 83. *Pastel.*   *Mde. Lusignan.*

264. George III., King of England. Curious old portrait of that King. *Engraving.*   *Hon. Judge Baby.*

265. William IV., King of England, known before his accession to the Throne as William Henry, Duke of Clarence. Third son of George III. Born 1765, died 1837. *Colored Print.*   *Hon. Judge Baby.*

266. Galt, John. Born 1779, died 1839. An author of some distinction and the father of the Hon. A. T. Galt, Minister of Finance, Canada. Came to Canada in 1826, as commissioner of the Canada Land Company. Founded the town of Guelph, and the town of Galt is named after him. *Engraving.*   *Hon. Judge Baby.*

267. Marquis de Themines, Acting Viceroy of New France 1616 to 1618. *Engraving.*

268. Grant, Sir William, Attorney-General of the Province of Quebec, 1776 to 1784, with autograph. *Engraving.*

269. The Duke of York, 1790, with autograph. *Engraving.*

270. Jarvis, William, First Provincial Secretary of Upper Canada, 1810, with autograph. *Engraving.*

271. Hincks, Sir Francis, Finance Minister of the Dominion, 1870, with autograph. *Lithograph.*

272. Brant, Joseph, Mohawk Chief 1775, with autograph. Brant, John, his son, superintendent of the Six Nation Indians, with autograph. *Engraving.*

        Nos. 267 to 272 the gift of Alfred Sandham, Esq.

35

273. Clarke, John, Chief Factor of the Hudson Bay Company, son of Simon of the same service. *Original in oil.*
   George Durnford, Esq.

274. Heriot, Major-General, the Hon. Frederick George Born 1786, died 18:.?. Founder of Drummondville Major in the Canadian Voltigeurs 1812. *Oil.*
   J. C. H. Heriot, Esq.

275. Heriot, George, Deputy Post-Master General of Canada, 1799 to 1816. *Silhouette.* *J. C. H. Heriot, Esq.*

276. Canadian Exiles at Bermuda, 1838. *Photo.*

277. McGillvry, Wm. A member of the old Nor.-west Company. *Oil.*
   C. de Lery Macdonald and W. D. Lighthall, Esq., K.C.

278. Gobelin Tapestry. Interior of a castle kitchen.
   H. J. Tiffin, Esq.

279. Regimental colors of the 2nd Battalion Mounted Royal Volunteers, Colonel the Hon. John Molson, 1837.
   John Molson, Esq.

280. Maquette of the Maisonneuve Monument, by the talented sculptor Hebert. *Comte de la Barthe.*

281. Bust of Hon. L. J. Papineau. *Vide No.* 200.
   E. Meloche, Esq.

282. Model of the Chenier Monument. Dr. J. Olivier Chenier, a young French Canadian *patriote*, killed at St. Eustache in 1837, while opposing the English troops.
   Dr. Louis Laberge.

283. Flag of the Loyal Beauharnois Volunteers, carried during the Rebellion 1837-38. It belonged to Col. Jonathan Odell, founder of Odelltown, U.E. Loyalist and officer in the militia in the war of 1812.
   Mrs. Lt.-Col. Arch. McEachern.

284. Jack of Lord Wolsey's flag. This Jack formed part of the Flag of the leading boat of Sir Garnet Wolsey's Expedition to the Red River, against Riel in 1870. On the English Regulars and Canadian Volunteers taking possession of Fort Garry, it was hoisted on the flag staff of the Fort. It was brought back by W. D. Dickinson, of the Royal Artillery, in whose possession it remained until his death in 1872.
   Mrs. Richardson Richards.

285. Flag carried by the Patriots in the Insurrection of 1837.
   Victor Morin, Esq.

286. Wooden figure of Governor Sir George Prevost, made by a soldier stationed at l'Assomption in 1812. Used as a sign by a country hotel for more than ninety years.
By Purchase.

CASE 1.

ANTIQUITIES.

1. Sword of Col. Pierre Guy, who was among those who signed the capitulation of Montreal with the Americans, 1775.
2. Sword of the Hon. Col. Frs. Baby, Adjutant-General of Militia, 1800.
3. French sword blades found on the Plains of Abraham.
4. Sword of Sir Guy Carleton, Lord Dorchester, Governor-General of Canada 1766 to 1796.
5. Sword of General Haldimand. Lieut.-Governor of Canada, 1778 to 1784.
6. Sword worn by Chas. De Lanaudiere, aide-de-camp to Lord Dorchester, when he was presented to Frederick the Great, along with Lieutenant de St. Ours, May 12, 1785.
7. Sword worn by Lieutenant St. Ours when he was presented to Frederick the Great, with Lieutenant de Lanaudiere, May 12, 1785.
8. Sword of an American officer in General Arnold's Division, taken at the assault on Quebec, Dec. 31, 1775.
9. Sword blade of Lacorne de St. Luc, Knight of St. Louis. Took Fort Clinton, 1747. Fought at Carillon and St. Foy.
10. The renowned Indian warrior Tecumseh's dagger.
11. Highlander's dirk from Plains of Abraham.
Nos. 1 to 11 presented by the Hon. Judge Baby.
12. Old horse pistol used at the Battle of Chateauguay, Oct. 24, 1813, by Captain Vital Dumouchel.
J. A. Dumouchel, Esq.
13. Old horse pistol, carried in the war of 1812.
Hon. Judge Baby.
14. Old pistol, flint lock, found at Lake Calumet.
Thos. O'Leary, Esq.
15. Toy cannon, belonging to J. B. F. Deschamps de Boishebert, 1646-1703. *G. D. de Boishebert, Esq.*
16. Two old cap pistols, English make, about 1840.
James Milloy, Esq.

17. Gorgets and breast plate, Canadian Militia.
18. Gorget of the Hon. Col. Frs. Baby, Adjutant-General of Militia.
19. Gorget of Col. de Salaberry, Canadian Volunteers.
20. Regiment ' breastplate of the Colonel of one of the French Regiments worn at Carillon.
21. Crossguns, Artillery officer's badge, found on the Plains of Abraham.
22. Button, Quebec Militia, 1775.
23. Button, Fire-Police, Montreal.
24. Button, 100th Royal Canadian Regiment.
25. Card with six buttons, Royal Canadian Volunteers.
26. Card with Regimental buttons found upon the demolition of St. Louis Gate, Quebec, in 1871.
 Nos. 17 to 26 presented by the Hon. Judge Baby.
27. Old-time badge of a Montreal carter.
 P. O. Tremblay, Esq.
28. Breast plate and knipple cleaners.
 A. Desroches, Esq.
29. Spoon found at Annapolis (Port Royal).
 R. W. McLachlan, Esq.
30. Pistol, belonged to Captain Rolette; carried during the war of 1812.
31. Pistol, blonged to General James Murray, first English Governor of Quebec, 1759-63.
32. Small birch bark basket, made by Indians, belonged to Madame D'Amours de Clignancourt, 1768.
33. *Porte-carafe*, birch bark with the arms of Tarieu de Lanaudiere, 1796.
34. Three medallions, Innocent IK., Emperor Claudius, and Emperor Domitian.
 Nos. 30 to 34 presented by the Hon Judge Baby.
35. Gold button from the uniform of Michel d'Irumberry de Salaberry, officer of the French Frigate " l'Anglesea," in 1735. He was the first of the name in Canada.
 Miss de Salaberry.
36. Button. The Royal Academy of Music, London, Worn by Mr. Mason, 1832. *Alfred Mason, Esq.*
37. Sword buckles worn by Girod, leader of the Patriots of 1837, at St. Benoit. He committed suicide to escape capture.

38. Bark jewel box made by Indians, belonged to Mme. Legardeur de Montesson, 1764.
Hon. Judge Baby.
39. Button from the uniform of Major Saml. David, Brigade Major, Montreal Militia, 1812-14.
S. David, Esq.
40. Pocket-book of General James Murray, Governor of Quebec, 1759-62, Governor-General of Canada, 1763-66.
Hon. Judge Baby.
41. Wooden back comb, carved by an Indian.
42. Ancient tortoise-shell glasses.
43. Antique necklet.
44. Valentine over a hundred years old.
45. Very old snuff box. *Late Mrs. H. Saunders.*
46. Card-case. A souvenir presented by Madame General Baronne de Riedesel, to Madame Francois Baby, nee Marie-Anne Tarieu de Lanaudiere, in 1786.
47. Note book of Sieur de la Verendrye, the explorer of the North West, and discoverer of the Rocky Mountains in 1731.
48. Card-case, belonged to Baroness de Germain, nee Le Moyne de Longueuil.
49. Two pistols that belonged to Dr. C. A. Theller, who, with several others, escaped from the Citadel of Quebec, by dropping over the walls, during the night of the 25th October, 1838.
50. Jubilee stamp, Prince of Wales Hospital, 1897.
51. Sheath for small scissors, 1745.
Nos. 46 to 51 presented by the Hon. Judge Baby.
52. Key plate from the door of Pope Innocent VI.'s room in the Fort St. Andre, Villeneuve-les-Avignon, France, built in 1226. *W. C. Palmer, Esq.*
53. Tassel from the Throne of Louis-Philippe, picked up at the sacking of the Tuilleries, 1848, by Guillaume Lamothe, Esq., late Postmaster of Montreal.
Hon. Judge Baby.
54. Teeth extractors used in Canada in the seventeenth century. *A. Desroches, Esq.*
55. Leaden plate from weather vane of Recollet Church.
O. Frappier, Esq.

56. Piece of furniture covering of the Blue Room in the Castle St. Louis, Quebec, destroyed by fire in 1834.
57. Piece of a cedar beam from the Castle St. Louis, Quebec. *Mrs. Robert Reid.*
58. Card, invitation issued by Lady Aylmer for a reception in the Chateau, June 23, 1831. *F. J. Audet, Esq.*
59. Sand box, used before the advent of blotting paper, brought from France by Pierre Guy, in 1727.
Hon. Judge Baby.
60. Piece of oak from Jacques-Cartier's vessel "La Petite Hermine," abandoned by him at Quebec in 1535, and discovered in 1845. *Hon. Judge Baby.*
60½. A piece of stone from the wall of Jacques-Cartier's House at Limoilu, near St. Malo, France, taken out by the donor, 1904. *C. de Salaberry, Esq.*
61. Two small boxes made from the woodwork of the tower of the old Notre-Dame Parish Church, which was on the Place-d'Armes, Montreal; pulled down in 1843.
S. M. Baylis, Esq.
62. Seal of the Seminary of St. Sulpice, Montreal, 1832.
J. A. U. Beaudry, Esq.
63. Piece of an oak tree that grew in the Jesuits' garden, opposite the Chateau, presented to the donor by Commandant Viger. *Hon. Judge Baby.*
64. Silver snuffers, belonged to Lady Johnson, wife of Sir John Johnson. *Hon. Judge Baby.*
65. Old-time flint and steel for lighting fires.
Jos. Lafontaine, Esq.
66. Eye-glasses, belonged to Madame Le Comte St. Georges Dupre, nee Marie-Louise Curot. *Hon. Judge Baby.*
67. Spectacles of Jos. Sherer, born at Levis, 1796.
Jos. Sherer, Esq.
68. Spectacles, belonged to the Hon. Louis Guy, 1838.
Hon. Judge Baby.
69. Old Masonic jewels, worn in the early part of the last century, in Canada. *Hon. Judge Baby.*
70. Brass spikes from the steamboat St. Lawrence 1844.
J. E. Buchanan, Esq.
71. Piece of the handcuffs taken off Davignon and Desmarais, the prisoners of 1837, who were rescued by Bonaventure Viger, on the Chambly Road.
Judge L. W. Sicotte.

72. Key of General Murray's room in the Old Bishop's Palace, Quebec, in 1759. *R. C. Lyman, Esq.*
73. Key of the first Theatre Royal, St. Paul street, Montreal, *Mrs. Robert Reid.*
74. Antique watch, once the property of Sir John Calvert, later Lord Baltimore. *Mr. Ohman.*
75. Watch belonging to Peter McLee, of Perthshire, Scotland, purchased in 1785. *Peter Macfarlane, Esq.*
76. Cross found in the field at St. Lambert, similar to ones given to the Indians by the early missionaries.
P. M. Wickham, Esq.
77. A Pass through the lines, issued by Philippe Gagnon, Riel's Secretary, during the rebellion of 1855.
P. O. Tremblay, Esq.

MINIATURES, etc.

78. De Salaberry-Ignace-Michel-Lonis-Antoine d'Irumberry, born at the Manor house, Beauport, July 5, 1752. Educated in France. Distinguished himself in 1775. A friend of the Duke of Kent, and father of the Hero of Chateauguay. Died March 22, 1825. (See 14, 55, 79, 80, 81.)
Original miniature on ivory.
79. De Salaberry, Marie-Anne Hertel de Rouville, born 1788, daughter of Hon. J. B. Melchior de Rouville, and wife of the " Hero of Chateauguay." (See 78.)
Original miniature on ivory.
80. Salaberry, Col. Hon. Charles-Michel-d'Irumberry de, "The Hero of Chateauguay." *See No. 14, Elgin Gallery.* (See 78.)
Original miniature on ivory. *By Subscription.*
81. Richmond, Charles Lennox, Duke of Richmond, Lennox, and Aubigny, K.G. *See portrait, 123, Elgin Gallery.*
Original miniature on ivory.
82. Daguerreotype copy of two oil portraits of the Panet family. *Hon. Judge Baby.*
83. Captain Francis Jackson.
Original miniature on ivory.
J. A. U. Beaudry, Esq.
84. Cugnet, Francois-Joseph, the younger.
Original miniature on snuff-box painted in Paris.
W. D. Lighthall, Esq., K. C.

85. La Fayette, Marquis de, commanding the Paris Militia, 1789. Presented to B. Joliette, at l'Assumption, Dec. 21, 1819.

86. Christie, Robert, M.P.P. A Canadian Historian. Was a native of Nova Scotia, but for a lengthened period a resident of Quebec. Born in 1788, died at Quebec 1856.
   Original miniature on ivory.   Hon. Judge Cimon.

87. Mondelet, Jean-Marie, notary, Father of the two Judges Mondelet.
   Original miniature on ivory.   By Subscription.

88. De Longueuil, Charles William Grant, 5th Baron, son of David Alexander Grant and the Baroness de Longueuil. Born at Quebec, February 4, 1782, died at Alwington House, Kingston, July 5, 1848. Was Legislative Councillor. (See 89 and Salon 1, 2, 3.)
   Original miniature on ivory.   Hon. Judge Baby.

89. Grant, William, brother of the 5th Baron de Longueuil. They were the only two male children of the Baroness Le Moyne de Longueuil. (See 88.)
   Original miniature on ivory.   Hon. Judge Baby.

90. M. l'Abbe de Beaujeu, confessor to Louis XVI. of France; was born in Canada.

91. De Beaujeu Amedee. Born at Paris, 1788. When quite young was attached to Napoleon's guard, known as *Gendarmes d'Ordonnance.*
   After distinguishing himself at the battles of Austerlitz, 1805; Jeno, 1806; Wagram, 1809, he perished in the ill-fated campaign of 1812.   *Mme. de Beaujeu.*

92. Louis-Joseph-Porlier Lamare. Born 1734. Married to Marie-Joseph Le Comte Dupre. Died Sept. 21, 1767.
   Original miniature on ivory.   By Subscription.

93. M. and Madame Lafontaine (Silhouette.) Born 1765 and 1775 respectively.   *Hon. Judge Baby.*

94. Head of The Saviour, miniature painting with carved wooden frame, formerly belonging to the Countess de Rastoul, of Avignon, France.   *W. C. Palmer, Esq.*

95. Portrait of M. de Gaspe, father of the author of "*Les Anciens Canadians,*" 1809. *Silhouette.*

96. Portrait of Jacques du Perron Baby, founder of the branch of the Baby family in Ontario. *Silhouette.*
   Hon. Judge Baby.

97. French rapier, found near Aultsville, in 1840.
   James Croil, Esq.

98. Old silver watch, found while digging a well near Chateauguay. *S. Bloomfield, Esq.*
99. Maule, Col. Lauderdale, of the 79th Highlanders at Quebec and Montreal. 2nd son of Lord Panmure, Minister of War of Great Britain, 1854. *Daguerreotype.*

CASE 2.

MEDALS OF THE POPES.

1. One hundred and eighty-five Papal medals, from St. Linus, who died in the year sixty-seven, to Leo XIII., 1903.
2. Twenty-five medals of Cardinals and others.
3. Medals of the Kings of France. (These medals were struck by order of Charles IK., King of France). From Pharamond, who reigned in 420, to Louis Philippe, 1830.
4. Collection of Canadian and Foreign Medals. Unclassified.
5. The silver medal and Khedive bronze medal awarded to Quartermaster Remington of the Canadian Nile contingent. *H. J. Tiffin, Esq.*
6. Cross of the Order of St. Louis, presented to Philippe de Rigaud, Marquis de Vaudreuil, Governor-General of New France, 1703 to 1725, by Louis KIV. of France.
Countess Cleremont-Tonnerre.
7. Beaver Club, Montreal. Instituted 1785. This exceedingly rare gold medal belonged to Robert Henry, 1793.
By Purchase.
8. Medal of the Beaver Club, rare Gold Medal, belonged to Gabriel Cote, 1796.
Loaned by C. A. Laframboise, Esq.
9. Silver Medal, Napoleon III., Empereur, L'Exposition Universelle de 1867, a Paris. *Hon. Judge Baby.*
10. Bronze Medal, Louis KIV.
11. Bronze Medal, *Republique Francais*, inscribed: "Au Musee, Chateau Ramezay, 1901."
The above two medals presented by L. Herbette, Esq., Paris.
12. Medal presented by the York Pioneers to the Rev. Henry Scadding, D.D., on the completion of Toronto of Old.
13. Tercentenary Medal of the founding of Quebec in 1608 by Samuel de Champlain. Presented by the National Battlefield Commission.

14. Medal commemorating the tercentenary of the discovery of Lake Champlain.
15. The Hudson-Fulton Centennial Medal.

A. Chausse, Esq.

CASE 3.

ABORIGINAL ANTIQUITIES.

This case contains Indian antiquities found by the Hon. Ed. Murphy in 1860, between Mansfield and Metcalfe streets, a little south of Sherbrooke street, on the site of the Indian Village of Hochelaga described by Jacques-Cartier in 1535.

Presented by the family of the late Hon. Senator Murphy.

CASE 4.

A collection of Canadian and Foreign Coins. Unclassified.

CASE 5.

Early printed books, also a collection of the first Canadian magazines.

1. Plan of Fort Duquesne. Captain Robert Stobo drew this plan whilst a prisoner or hostage at Fort Duquesne after the capture of Fort Necessity in 1754. He had the plan conveyed to the commanding officer at Wills' Creek. His correspondence fell into the hand of the French on the defeat of General Braddock, and he was consequently committed to prison at Quebec, whence he attempted to escape in 1756, but was overtaken and brought back, and was afterwards tried on a charge of treason and sentenced to be beheaded, but the sentence was not put into execution. He made a second attempt to escape, but was again brought back; in 1758 he made a third attempt and succeeded in joining the British Army at Louisbourg. He accompanied it to Quebec where he was very useful to the English by his knowledge of the localities.
2. View of the Battle of Odelltown, where 1200 insurgents were defeated with less than 200 of Her Majesty's Loyal Volunteers, 9th Nov. 1838.

Mrs. R. L. Rolland.

3. Lacolle Mill and Blockhouse, where Major Handcock with 340 regulars and militia repulsed the American General Wilkinson and army of 4000 and 3 cannon, March 30, 1814. *G. M. Van Fleet, Esq.*

44

4. Document signed by Governor de Ramesay, 1719.
Sheriff Lemieux.

5. A pair of saddle pistols, and a pair of XVIII Century pistols. Belonged to J. F. Perrault of Quebec, used by his father when travelling as a fur trader.
Madame Perrault-Casgrain.

6. A mummy Ibis brought from Egypt by the donor.
Victor Morin, Esq.

7. A lamp from the tombs outside Nablus, Palestine, supposed to be of the third century, B.C.
George Wride Strawson, Esq., Eng.

8. Ivory Crucifix in carved gilt frame, Louis XIV. period from the Taschereau (Desrivieres) Household, Quebec.
W. D. Lighthall, Esq., K.C.

CASE 6.

INDIAN ANTIQUITIES.

1. Sheath for knife, worked in beads.

   Sheath for knife, worked in porcupine quills.

3. Wrist bands, arm bands and collars, beautifully worked in beads.

4. Four buckskin tobacco pouches, ornamented in various styles.

5. Card, arrowheads and Indian pipes beautifully carved, done by Indians in the North-West.

6. Stem for pipe, in fancy work.

7. Horsewhip with double lash, ornamented handle.
The foregoing presented by Hon. Judge Baby.

8. Indian war club or "casse-tete," worked in wood.
G. de Boishebert, Esq.

9. Indian club or "casse-tete," worked in wood.
H. J. Tiffin, Esq.

9½. Indian "casse-tete," iron. *Hon. Judge Baby.*

10. Tobacco pipe belonged to "Poundmaker," a celebrated Indian Chief of the North-West.

11. Tobacco pouch belonged to "Crowfoot," also a noted Indian Chief of the North-West. *Dr. J. W. Mount.*

12. A Chief's pouch, transparent beads, finely worked on cloth. Sioux tribe. *H. J. Tiffin, Esq.*

13. Square of Indian bead work done on buckskin.
    A. Sandham, Esq.
14. Chilcat Indian medicine man's head-dress, mother-of-pearl and shell ornaments, from Alaska.
15. Medicine man's rattle to drive off evil spirits.
16. British Columbia Indian gambling game. Very old and interesting. *H. J. Tiffin, Esq.*
17. Earthenware pot found in the vicinity of Lake Edward. Rarely seen in such perfect condition.
    Hon. Judge Baby.
18. String of shell wampum from Queen Charlotte Islands.
19. Necklet of wampum from same place.
    H. J. Tiffin, Esq.
20. Indian wampum.
21. Hand mangle, made of bone.
22. Alaska Indian fish hook.
23. Horn spoon, Chilcat Indians. *H. J. Tiffin, Esq.*
24. Carved drinking cup, made from a piece of maple by a *Tete-de-Boule* Indian, inhabiting the head waters of the St. Maurice. *Geo. B. Day, Esq.*
25. Stone hide scraper. *W. A. Ryan, Esq.*
26. Chilcat Indian's smoking pipe, carved to represent a whale. *H. J. Tiffin, Esq.*
27. A "*Gibeciere*," or pouch, made by Indians of the Mackenzie River and given to Mgr. Cote.
    Hon. Judge Baby.
28. Skull of a Pagan Indian (apparently pre-historic Hochelagan). Found with others in a burying place on the site of Mount Royal Cemetery, about 1850.
    Geo. B. Day, Esq.
29. Skeleton of a young Indian girl of pre-historic times. Found (Sept., 1898) in an old Indian burying ground at Westmount. Considered to be of the Hochelaga Indians, whose town was visited by Jacques Cartier in 1535. It was found in the position in which the bones are now placed knees drawn up as usual in Indian burials.
    W. D. Lighthall, Esq., K.C.
30. War spear, belonged to "Crowfoot," a noted Indian Chief of the North-West.
31. Tooth of a Mastodon brought from Alaska, by Mercier, the well-known traveller of the Polar Regions.
    Hon. Judge Baby.

46

32. Three skulls of Indians, dug up at Westmount in 1898.
W. D. Lighthall, Esq., K.C.

CASE 7

DOCUMENTS.

1. Documents relating to the Seniory of *Ste. Anne de la Perade* in 1710.
2. Documents signed by Adhemar, second Royal Notary of Montreal, 1675.
3. Document signed by Intendant Raudot, 1710.
4. Document signed by Intendant Begon, 1726.
5. Document signed by Delino, Royal Notary, 1728.
6. Document signed by Monseignat, *Conseil Superieur*.
7. Document signed by Intendant Hocquart, 1735.
The above the gift of J. J. Gibb, Esq.
8. Document signed by Audouart, the first Notary at Quebec, 1651.
9. Document signed by Governor de Lauzon, 1662.
10. Document signed by Pierre Boucher, Governor of Three Rivers, 1662.
11. Document signed by Intendant Begon, 1723.
12. Document signed by Intendant Dupuis, 1728.
The above from Huguet-Latour, Esq.
13. Autograph of Jean-Baptiste-Roch de Ramezay, son of Governor Claude de Ramezay. He signed the Capitulation of Quebec, 1759.
14. Autograph of l'abbe E. Montgolfier, priest of the Seminary of St. Sulpice, Montreal, and brother of the celebrated inventors of the balloon.
Hon. Judge Baby.
15. An order given after the Cession of the Colony, for money to be paid to Sieur Perthius, formerly *Procureur du Roi*, signed by le Duc de Choiseul, 1763.
C. de Lery Macdonald, Esq.
16. Envelopes of the 18th century, bearing address of Canadian officers. *Hon. Judge Baby.*
17. Lithograph copy of a grant of land in Quebec, made by the Company of the Hundred Associates, to Abraham Martin (Plains of Abraham), dated 1635.
John Reade, Esq.

18. Photograph of a document, deed of sale from Captain de la Forest to Michel Aco, 1693.
19. Lithograph copy of a document, grant made by de la Salle to Michel Disy, signed by " La Salle."
    The Hon. Justice Girouard.
20. Autograph letter of Benedict Arnold, Commander-in-Chief of the American Army at Pointe-aux-Trembles, near Quebec, Nov. 28, 1775.
    L. N. Dumouchel, Esq.
21. Judgment given in the Court of Common Pleas, District of Quebec, 1777.
22. Document relating to the Seigniory of Dorvilliers, signed by Governor Haldimand, 1781.
23. Autograph letter of General Gabriel Christie. Was an officer under Wolfe.
24. Autograph of John Jacob Astor (founder of the Astor family), when in business in Mc   1796.
25. Handbill giving notice of the escape of three American prisoners of war from the Lower Bijou, near Quebec.
26. Letters of Colonel T. Coffin relating to the foregoing prisoners.
27. Description of three American officers, prisoners of war who escaped from Quebec. September 27, 1814.
28. Muster roll of 2nd Company of Nicolet Militia, July 11, 1814.
29. Autograph letter of Sir James Kempt, 1827.
30. Autograph letter of Sir Charles Bagot, Governor-General, 1842.
31. Documents bearing the autographs of the following Governors-General of Canada:—
    Robert Shorle Milnes, Lieut-Governor, 1799.
    J. Monk, President of the Council, 1819.
    Lord Dalhousie, 1827.
    Lord Gosford, 1837.
    Sir John Colborne, Lord Seaton, 1838.
    Lord Sydenham, 1841.
    Lord Cathcart, 1846.
    Lord Elgin and Kincardine (2) 1847-48.
    William Rowan, C.B., Administrator, 1853.
    Sir Edmund Walker Head, 1858.
    Lord Monck, 1862.
    Sir John Young, 1870.

32. Order, signed by L. J. Papineau, Speaker of the House, that the Sergeant-at-arms take into custody N. Aubin, who, with P. A. de Gaspe, had sprinkled assafoetida in the wardrobes in the House of Assembly, on February 13, 1836.
  Nos. 21 to 32 presented by the Hon. Judge Baby.
33. Pay list of St. Eustache Volunteer Regiment of Foot, December, 1838. *W. Seath, Esq.*
34. Facsimile of a fly sheet found under a cairn in the Arctic regions, deposited by Polar expedition of the "Erebus and Terror," commanded by Sir John Franklin. *Alfred Pinsonneault, Esq.*
35. Documents signed by Lieutenant-Governor R. S. Milnes, 1804; Sir George Prevost, 1812; Sir James Kempt, 1825; Lord Monck, 1864; Jacques Viger, first Mayor of Montreal. *Huguet-Latour, Esq.*
36. Journal writen on birch bark, by Jean Steinbruck, of the North-West Company, during 1802-03.
  Hon. Louis R. Masson.
37. Journal of Thomas Vercheres de Boucherville in an expedition to the North-West, in 1803, also during the war of 1812-13. *Hon. Judge Baby.*
38. Last letter written by Chevalier de Lorimier, a few hours before his execution, 1839.
39. Original programme of Amateur Performance, Theatre Royal, Montreal, May 28, 1842, in which Charles Dickens took part. *Mrs. Henry Hogan.*
40. Document signed by Catherine de Medicis, 1554.
41. Deed, signed by Louis Philippe, Duc d'Orleans (Philippe Egalite), at the Palais Royal, Paris, May 1, 1781.

CASE 8.

OLD CHINA, ETC.

1. Punch bowl brought from India by Michael Gratz, Esq., in 1739. *Mrs. Sarah Gratz Joseph.*
2. Two old bowls used in the family of Sir Walter Scott, at Abbotsford, in 1787. *Miss Macfarlane.*
3. Side dish, belonged to the McKensie family of Terebonne.
4. Small dish, belonged to the family of Jacques Hervieux, 1764.

5. Dish, belonged to Madame Louise de la Corne de Chapt, nee Marie-Anne Hervieux, 1742.
6. Sauce bowl, willow pattern, 1750.
7. Dinner plate, family of Sir John Johnson, 1784.
8. Plate, belonged to the McGill family, James McGill, the founder of McGill University.
9. Small Plate, 1760.
10. Soup plate of the dc Ramesay family, 1700. In use in the Chateau two hundred years ago.
11. Plate of the Frobisher family, 1791.
    Nos. 3 to 11 presented by the Hon. Judge Baby.
12. Plate of the Rastel de Rocheblave family, 1754.
    Miss de Rocheblave.
13. Nest of French brass weights, small.
14. Nest of brass weights, large size. In use in 1730.
15. Scale and weights, used by merchants to weigh gold and silver, 1732.
16. Scale and weights, used by medical gentlemen in 1730.
17. Antique coffee pot.
18. Antique Canadian shaving mug in pewter.
19. Very old cover dish, embossed copper.
20. Antique "*Rechaud*," belonged to the family of Denys de la Ronde, 1694.
21. Very old "*casserole*," belonged to the Panet-Cerre family, 1784.
22. Ancient French wafer-iron (*gaufrier*), belonged to the Guy family, in 1737.
    Nos. 14 to 22 presented by the Hon. Judge Baby.
23. Very old stone saucer, Q.L.A.   *J. B. Emberson, Esq.*
24. Old English pitcher, with the farmer's creed.
    Jos. Broughton, Esq.
26. "*Casserole*," in copper. Belonged to Mlle de Lagauchetiere.
27. "*Casserole*," in copper. Belonged to Mlle Denys de Vitre, 1728.
28. Bronze mortar. Belonged to Sieur Jean-Francois. Gauthier, King's surgeon and member of the *Conseil Superieur*, discoverer of *Gaultheria prociembens*, 1754.

29. Piece of slate from roof of Chateau de Vaudreuil, Montreal.

No. 26 to No. 29 presented by the Hon. Judge Baby.

30. Piece of slate from the Montcalm house, Quebec.
Mrs. J. Welch.

31. Lead plate found in foundation stone of an old building on St. Paul street, 1721.

32. Copper flint-box with embossed heads of seven different kings, 16th century. *H. J. Tiffin, Esq.*

33. Miniature siege gun made out of stone of the Malakoff Fort, and brought to Canada by Chs. Buckley, Esq., M.D., who served in the Crimean War as surgeon, together with several other Canadians. Presented by his daughter. *Miss Josephine Buckley.*

34. Antique ivory sand box, used before the advent of blotting paper. *Hon. Judge Baby.*

35. Norsman's knife-sheath, elaborately carved, bearing date 1497. *H. J. Tiffin, Esq.*

36. Tea caddy, belonged to Mrs. Simon McTavish, nee Marguerite Chaboillez, 1794.

37. Pair of crimson velvet ball shoes, embroidered in gold. Worn in 1750; belonged to the de Beaujeu family.

38. Pair of white satin ball-shoes, worn in 1754; belonged to the de Beaujeu family.

39. White satin ball shoes, belonged to Mme Chs. X. Tarieu de Lanaudiere, nee Genevieve Deschamps de Boishebert, 1758, grand-daughter of Claude de Ramezay, Governor of Montreal. *Hon. Judge Baby.*

40. Ball slippers. Belonged to Mme de Chapt de St-Luc Lacorne, nee Hervieux. *Mlle Baby.*

41. Ball slippers. Worn by Mlle Le Compte St. George Dupre, when she danced with H.R.H. the Duke of Kent at a ball in the Castle St. Louis, Quebec, in 1791.

42. Ball slippers, belonged to the same.
Donated by Mde Parant.

43. Pincushion, owned by Madam Pierre Guy, in 1737.
Hon. Judge Baby.

44. Epaulettes of Col. Hon. John Molson, commanding the 2nd Battalion of Montreal Volunteers, 1837.
John Molson, Esq.

45. Antique carved box, which belonged to the Comte de Douglas, who was allied to the de Ramezay family.
46. Two tortoise shell back combs. Worn by Canadian ladies about 1800.
47. Brass door knocker, from 'the " Berri " house, which belonged to the Hon. Louis Guy, 1839.
48. A perfume box. *Hon. Judge Baby.*
49. Silver trowel used in the laying of the corner stone of the Maisonneuve monument, 1893.
50. Bronze inkstand which belonged to Sir George E. Cartier. *Presented by Sir Wilfrid Laurier.*
51. Letters Patent of Knighthood of Sir Geo. E. Cartier, with the Great Seal of England attached. 52. His chapeau. 53. Bronze candlestick, and 54. A nest of brassweights. *Presented by J. E. Lusignan, Esq.*

DE VAUDREUIL ROOM.

1. McAlpine, The Reverend, Cousin of Gen. Gabriel Christie, and tutor to his family. *Oil.*
2, 3, 4. Sons of General Gabriel Christie. *Oil.*
5. Christie, William, a brother of Gen. Christie, died 1799. *Oil.*
6. Wellington, Arthur Wellesley, Duke of.
   Born in Ireland, May 1, 1769. Died in London, Sept. 18, 1852. The greatest general recorded in British History. Defeated Napoleon at Waterloo, June 18, 1815.
   Original in oil. *James Morgan, Esq.*
7. Napoleon Bonaparte.
   Born at Ajaccio, in Corsica, Feb. 5, 1768. Died at St. Helena, May 5, 1821. Was one of the greatest generals of any age, defeated every nation of Europe, with the exception of England, became Emperor of France, but after his defeat at Waterloo was exiled to St. Helena. In 1841 his remains were remov d to France and were interred under the dome of the nvalides. i
   Original by David. *James Morgan, Esq.*
8. Small, Major-General, John. Governor of Guernsey, Channel Islands. A Lieutenant in the 42nd, Royal Highland Black Watch, at the Battle of Carillon, 1758, and afterwards Colonel of 2nd Battalion Royal Highland Emigrants. He led a column at the Battle of Bunker Hill. *Pastel.* *By Subscription.*
9, 10. M. La Ber and wife, nee Hamilton. Le Ber was a prominent Montreal merchant in the early part of last century. *Oil.* *Miss J. Macdonald.*

11. Portrait of Arent Schuyler de Peyster. Major and Lieut.-Colonel in the 8th or King's Regiment of Foot, 1777-93; Colonel in the British Army, 1793; Colonel 1st Regiment Dumfries Volunteers, 1796. *Engraving.*
12. John Watts, last Royal Recorder of the City of New York, 1775. Born ,27th August, 1749; died, 13th Sept., 1836. *Engraving.*   *W. D. Lighthall, Esq., K.C.*
13. Lake Superior, a "misty morning."
   Painted by E. Hopkins. Engraved by Mottram.
14. Parchment document bearing the signature of Bishop Laval, 1688 (the first bishop of New France).
15. Concession par les Rev. Peres de St-Sulpice a Pierre Godbois, signee 1670, par l'abbe de Quelus.
16. Original subscription list for the Citizens' Ball given to Commander de Belveze and officers of the French corvette *La Capricieuse*, July, 1855.
   Nos. 2 to 4 presented by Judge L. W. Sicotte.
17. Piece of the flag presented to the Canadian militia, by Lady Dorchester, in 1775.   *Maurice Panet, Esq.*
18. Notarial agreement of Frs. Huster, to serve in the Canadian Voltigeurs, 10th Dec., 1812.
   Judge L. W. Sicotte.
19. Old play bill for performance at Mr. J. Durant's New Market (now Jacques Cartier Square), Sept. 9, 1818.
   L. N. Dumouchel, Esq.
20. Very old map of Florida and Natives.
   Hon. Judge Baby.
21. Photograph of an original Viking ship from Gogstad.
   C. T. Hart, Esq.
22. Petition of the Seigneurs, Magistrates, Members of the Clergy, Officers of Militia, Land Owners, and other Inhabitants of Lower Canada, 21st Nov., 1822.
   Hon. Judge Baby.

23. The coronation of Queen Victoria, June 28, 1838.
24. Marriage of Queen Victoria, Feb., 1840.
   H. J. Tiffin, Esq.
25. Steel engraved portrait of Her Late Majesty Queen Victoria in 1846.
26. Steel engraved portrait of His Late Royal Highness The Prince Consort, 1847.   *Hon. Judge Baby.*
27. Deed naming M. Masthod as a Baron of France, signed by Napoleon I. at Fontainebleau, 6th Oct., 1810.

28. Descriptive chart of the customs of the natives of Canada, by Pere Henepin, 1711. *H. J. Tiffin, Esq.*
29. Illustrations from the life of Wm. Lyon McKenzie, leader of the insurrection in Upper Canada, 1837-38.
Fred. Hague, Esq., B.C.L.
30. Plan on parchment, of Fort Detroit, in 1760-63.
M. l'Abbe Ouellette.
31. Views:—Jacques-Cartier's house at Limoilu, near St. Malo, France: Discovering Canada; Landing at Quebec, 1535; and Conference with Donacona.
Hon. Judge Baby.
32. View of old French house at Sorel, occupied by H.R.H. the Duke of Kent, in 1794. *A. J. Rice, Esq.*
33. Symes, Robert. A Quebec merchant, being inaugurated as an honorary chief of the Huron Tribe of Indians, at Lorette, near Quebec, 1841. *Hon. Judge Baby.*
34. Present view of the field of Carillon or Ticonderoga (water color by the donor). *T. Henry Carter, Esq.*
35. Death of General Wolfe, battle of the Plains of Abraham, 13th Sept., 1759.
36. The death of the Great Wolfe, caricature, after Benj. West's death of Wolfe, by Gilray. *S. Carsley, Esq.*
37. Jacques-Cartier, in his first interview with the Indians of Hochelaga (now Montreal), in 1535.
John Morrice, Esq.
38. Proclamation of Sir James Henry Craig, Governor General of Canada, 22nd March, 1810.
Hon. Judge Baby.
39. Descriptive chart of the products and animals of Canada, by Pere Henepin, 1711. *Hon. Judge Baby.*
40. Photograph:—Landing of H.R.H. The Princess Louise and the Marquis of Lorne at Halifax from the R.M.S. "Sarmatian," also H.M.S. "Black Prince," Captain H.R.H. the Duke of Edinburgh, and H.M.S. "Northampton." *C. T. Hart, Esq.*
41. List of subscribers to St. Patrick's Dinner in 1835.
42. Paper money:—Bond of the Irish Republic, issued at New York; Bill of Exchange of English Bank; Cuban fractional note; United States fractional note; Canadian fractional note and Buenos Ayres note.
Hon. Judge Baby.

43. Interior view of Old Fort Garry, a vanished scene.
   H. J. Tiffin, Esq.
44. The flag of Carillon, blue print copy of this famous flag.
   E. Gagnon, Esq.
45. Montcalm entering Quebec, having been mortally wounded on the Plains of Abraham, 13th Sept. 1759.
46. Death of General Wolfe. Battle of the Plains of Abraham, 13th Sept., 1759.
47. Battle of the Plains of Abraham, curious old print showing the Highlanders scaling the Heights.
   Hon. Judge Baby.
48. Death of General Montgomery, before Quebec, Dec. 31, 1775. *S. Carsley, Esq.*
49. British Soldiers drawing wood, from St. Foy to Quebec, in the winter of 1759-60. *H. J. Tiffin, Esq.*
50. The last Great Council of the West. From the original painting in the possession of the Marquis of Lorne.
   H. J. Tiffin, Esq.
51. McDonough's victory on Lake Champlain, and the defeat of the British Army at Plattsburgh, by Gen. Macomb, Sept. 11, 1814. *Engraved by B. Tauner.*
   Published 4th July, 1816, at Philadelphia.
   Very rare copper-plate. *Hon. Judge Baby.*
52. Death of General Brock at the Battle of Queenston Heights, 13th Oct., 1812.
53. Battle of Queenston Heights, Oct. 13, 1812, which ended in a complete victory on the part of the British, having captured 927 men, killed or wounded about 500. Taken 1,400 stand of arms, a six-pounder and a stand of colors. *Rare old print.* *H. J. Tiffin, Esq.*
54. Battle of Queenston Heights, Oct. 13, 1812. *Rare old print.* Corresponds exactly with No. 47, with the exception that the position of the contending forces have been transposed. *Alfred Sandham, Esq.*
55. First Review of British Volunteers, The Metropolitan Rifle Corps, in Hyde Park, 1860.
56. Snow blockade on the G. T. Railway, at black River, 1869.
57. Snow blockade at Chaudiere, March, 1869.
58. G. T. R. Erection Shops, Point St. Charles, in 1860.
59. Officers of the G. T. Railway, 1860.

60. Directors and Superintendent, G. T. Railway, 1861.
61. H.M.S. "Aurora," Captain A. R. F. de Horsey, in winter quarters, St. Charles River, Quebec, 1866.
    The foregoing presented by C. T. Hart, Esq.
62. Plate, fac-simile of medals—British awards for valor on land and sea during the last fifty years.
    H. J. Tiffin, Esq.
63. The First Railway train to run in Canada, between Laprairie and St. John's, 1836.
    P. J. L'Heureux, Esq.
64. Fac-simile of the Magna-Charta, A.D. 1218. With the seals of the King's securities to Magna-Charta, and shields of ye Barons in Arms. *Eug. Lafontaine, Esq.*
65. Genealogical Chart of the family of Boufflers, 1167 to 1690. Beautifully illuminated work on parchment (*original*).
66. Confederation—The Members who composed the Quebec Convention in 1866.
67. Jubilee group. Patriots of 1837-38 and the Liberal Cabinet of the Province of Quebec, 1887-88.
    No. 64 to No. 67 presented by the Hon. Judge Baby.
68. Garden Party, Buckingham Palace, Queen's Jubilee, 1887.
69. The Jubilee celebration in Westminster Abbey, June 21, 1887. Commemorative of the fiftieth year of the Reign of Queen Victoria.
70. Wreck of H.M.S. "Birkenhead." The "Birkenhead" went down in 1852 with 500 officers and men, standing in the presence of death as calmly as on parade ground, whilst the women and children were saved.
    H. J. Tiffin, Esq.
71. G. T. R. Locomotive "Lady Elgin," built at Portland, in 1852. This locomotive operated in Upper Canada, May 16, 1853.
72. The "Toronto No. 2." First locomotive built at Toronto, by James Good, 1853.
73. Old locomotive built at Toronto, 1858.
    C. T. Hart, Esq.
74. King Charles I., of England, on the way to execution, Jan. 30, 1649. On the fatal day, attended by Dr. Juxon, Bishop of London, he was conducted on foot by a strong guard through St. James' Park to a scaffold erected in the open street before the banquetting house at Whitehall. *H. J. Tiffin, Esq.*

75. The Postman of the North.
Drawn from life by Arthur H. Heming.

76. The Louisbourg Bell. This bell was blessed in France and hung in the steeple of the Church at Louisbourg, in 1724. Upon the capitulation of the town, in 1758, it was carried to Halifax, and for many years was in St. John's Chapel at Three Mile House. In 1895 a subscription was raised in Montreal for its purchase and later it was presented to this Museum, through *Francoise*, Miss Barry.

CASE 9.

Contains a large collection of Indian Antiquities, consisting of stone axes, hammers, chisels, gouges, arrow-heads, bead work, pottery of various shapes, etc., etc.
Loaned by Major Piche.

CASE 10.

1. Relics from the ruins of Louisbourg. In 1758, Louisbourg was the strongest fortress in French or British America. Wrought iron nails from gun platforms, bolts, hinges, locks, keys, scissors, knives and forks, musket-bullets, horseshoes, oak pegs from the ship yard, etc. *H. J. Tiffin, Esq.*

2. Hatchet, from the ruins of Louisburg.
Hon. Arthur Boyer.

3. Fragment of a cannon ball from the ruins of Louisbourg.
S. M. Baylis, Esq.

4. Piece of the cannon that burst at Sohmer Park, 15th July, 1896, during the French fete.
Judge L. W. Sicotte.

5. Small bullet from the Plains of Abraham.
Hon. Judge Baby.

6. Grape shot found on the field after the Battle of St Charles, Nov. 25, 1837. *Mrs. J. H. Peck.*

7. Fragment of an exploded shell from Fort Oswego.

8. Fragment of an exploded shell from Fort Frontenac.
Hon. Judge Baby.

9. Fragment of exploded shell from Carillon.
W. D. Lighthall, Esq.

10. Iron staple from old French Fort at St. Johns, Que.
W. D. Lighthall, Esq.

11. Small double-barreled pistol of seventy years ago.
    R. B. Hall, Esq.

12. Bayonet from the ruins of Louisbourg. Presented to the donor by Dr. Almon, M.P., Halifax.

13. Bayonet found on the Plains of Abraham. Presented to the donor by Hon. P. J. O. Chauveau.

14. Bayonet from the Battle of St. Foy. Presented to the donor by Hon. J. G. Bosse. *Hon. Judge Baby.*

15. A Fenian bayonet, raid of 1870. *A. T. Taylor, Esq.*

16. Old bayonet, used in 1837 by donor's grandfather.
    Regis Picard, Esq.

17. Old bayonet, found on Cove Fields, Quebec.
    Thos. O'Leary, Esq.

18. Brass bullet mould, in use in 1837. *Lymburner, Esq.*

19. On card. Piece of brick from Fort Frontenac, piece of brick from Fort Naigara, piece of stone from Fort Oswego, arrowheads from Joliette, and one of the first cartridges made in Quebec. *Hon. Judge Baby.*

20. Key found on site of Old Bishop Palace, Quebec.
    P. J. Brennan, Esq.

21. Section of the first steel rail made at Sault Ste. Marie.
    Albert Lomas, Esq.

22. Fragments of an exploded shell picked up at St. Eustache the day after the battle, by the late James Ferrier. *Mrs. J. Ferrier.*

23. Grape shot, bullets, flints and nails from the ruins of Fort Ticonderoga. *A. G. Van Schaik, Esq.*

24. Door latch from the old barracks at Chateauguay.
    W. C. Palmer, Esq.

25. Three door hinges from the Chapel of Notre-Dame-de Victoire, built 1713, demolished in 1900.

26. Pieces of old iron articles found in the vaults by
    T. O'Leary, Esq.

27. Fragments of delftware found on opening the chimney in the vaults, 1895. *R. W. McLachlan, Esq.*

28. Small bombshell from Gaspe County.
    Pemberton Smith, Esq.

29. Snuff box carved out of a nut shell.
    L. N. Pare, Esq.

58

30. Old French lock, from the Lachance House, l'Assomption.
    L. Gauthier, Esq.
31. Old French lock.   *Messrs. Lapres & Lavergne.*
32. Old iron chain from the site of Chateau de Callieres.
    Jas. Currie, Esq.
33. Wooden carpenter's tools of Thomas Dahan, the pioneer of Melbourne Township. *P. Z. Milette, Esq.*
34. Special constable's baton, carried by R. L. Picard, at Napierville, in 1837.   *R. Picard, Esq.*
35. Government constable's baton of 1837.
36. Cane made from timber of the "Royal Sovereign," blown up at St. Johns, Que.   *M. Carleau.*
37. Cane made from timber of the "Royal George." The "Royal George," 108 guns, commanded by Admiral Kempenfeldt, filled and went down off Portsmouth, 29th Aug., 1782. Of the total of eleven hundred souls on board only about two hundred were saved.
    W. D. Lighthall, Esq. K. C.
38. Old door-bolt, from Chateau kitchen.
    Miss Gilmour.
39. Wooden wheel of a gun carriage, brought from England by Lord Selkirk, and placed in Fort Garry, 1810.
    Mrs. H. S. Lomas.
40. From Chateau Haldimand, Quebec, a piece of railing of the principal staircase, a piece of the cornice of reception room, a fragment of the paving of the Council room.   *Cyrille Tessier, Esq.*
41. Key-plate off a door in the Chateau.
42. Piece of mortar from the old Fortifications of Montreal, built in 1723.
43. Fused brass, found in ruins of Old Parliament House. Montreal, 1849, the morning after the fire.
    H. J. Ross, Esq.
44. Piece of wrought iron, from vault's windows.
45. Piece of stone from the old La Corne house, No. 309 St. Paul street.

CASE 11.

INDIAN ANTIQUITIES.

Loaned by R. W. McLachlan, Esq.

46. Fragments of pottery. Found on the site of Hochelaga, on Metcalfe street, near Sherbrooke street.

47. Fragment of pottery. Showing inside handle by which the vessel was suspended over the fire.
48. Fragment of a terra-cotta vessel. Hochelaga.
49. Small quoit made from a broken jar.
50. Clay bead.
51. Fragments of clay pipes. Hochelaga.
52. Stone hammer. "
53. Stone mashing knife. "
54. Stone axe.
55. Stone celt.
56. Stone gouge or tapper.
57. Flake.
58. Arrowhead. "
59. Bugle beads. Made from Lake Superior native copper, Hochelaga.
60. Stone instruments for tracing designs on pottery. Hochelaga.
61. Bone bodkin. Hochelaga.
62. Butternut. "
63. Charred corn cobs. "
64. Charred wood.
65. Fresh water unio shells. "
66. Fragments of human bones from Hochelaga.
67. Human bones from ancient burial places.
68. Fragments of pottery from Islands in the St. Lawrence, near Dundee.
69. Fragment of a clay pipe.
70 to 78. Stone celts or skinners. Hochelaga.
79. Fragment of a steatite pipe—Mound-builder's pattern. Hochelaga.
80. Flint arrowheads. Hochelaga.
81. Gouge or tapper. "
82. Fragment of a spear head. "
83. Gouge. St. Lawrence.
84. Small celt. "
85. Broken Iroquois spearhead from Auburn, N.Y.

86. Large arrowhead. St. Lawrence.
87. Six fine specimens of Wyandotte arrowheads from Norfolk Co., Ont.
88. Arrowhead from Trenton, Ont.
89. Rubbed arrowhead.
90. Broken Algonquin spearhead, from Clarence, Ont.
91. Algonquin quartz arrowhead.   "
92. Algonquin taper.   "
93. Algonquin celts.   "
94. Algonquin sandstone gouge from Buckingham.
95. Fragment of pottery made by Huron Indians, from Balsam, Lake Ontario.
96. Steatite pipes.
97. Clay pipe, snake pattern, from Bobcaygeon, Ont.
98. Copper chisel from Bridgeville, Ont.
99. Stone mattock from Wellington, Ont.
100. Stone mattock (Iroquois), from Auburn, N.Y.
101. Fine specimen of ancient British spearhead.
102. Fragments of a very large Pottery Jar, found on Sept., 1900, in a mound at Helena, N.Y.
W. D. Lighthall, Esq., K.C.
103. Indian arrowheads, flakes, chips and cores, found at Fort Ticonderoga (Carillon, May 24, 1897. Excursion of the Numismatic and Antiquarian Society.)
104. Arrowheads from Fort Ticonderoga.
W. D. Lighthall, Esq., K.C.
105. Stone celt or skinner, found at Hudson, P.Q.
T. B. Macaulay,
Presented by W. D. Lighthall, Esq., K.C.
106. Fragments of Indian pottery, found in Victoria County, Ont.
107. Fragments of Indian pottery from Prince Edward County, Ont.
108. Fragments of Indian pottery from Pickering Township, Ont.
109. Fragments of Indian pottery from Clerk Township, Durham Co., Ont.
110. Fragments of Indian pottery from Welland Co., On

111. Fragments of Indian pottery from Brant Co., Ont.
112. Fragments of pottery from the Mohawk Valley.
113. Fragments of pottery from Islands in the St. Lawrence, opposite Lancaster.

CASE 12.

INDIAN ANTIQUITIES.

1. Card containing relics found in an Indian grave at Lake Edward, north of Quebec.

   Card containing Indian amulets, necklace, etc., from Lake Edward.

3. Card containing Indian relics from an Indian grave at Lake Edward.   *Hon. Judge Baby.*

4. Stone hammer ..... adou
            C. de L. Macdonald, Esq.

5. Stone used for tapping maple trees.
            H. J. Tiffin, Esq.

   Stone used as a hammer.

7. Specimen of shell conglomerate from Florida.
            Miss D   d.

8. Piece of stone from which arrowheads were made.
9. Algonquin celt, from Repentigny.
10. Stone used as a hammer.
11. Mound-builder's celt. Ohio.   *H. J. Tiffin, Esq.*
1 Quartz and flint arrowheads from South Carolina.
12½. Broken arrowheads from Fort Ticonderoga.
            W. D. Lighthall, Esq., K.C.
13. 2 arrowheads from Pointe-du-Lac, near Three Rivers.
            R. W. McLachlan, Esq.

   Stone implement from Isle-du-Pas.   *L. Julien, Esq.*

   Mound builder's stone pestles. Ohio.

    Fragment of pottery from Florida.
18. Stone implement, from Ohio.
19. Stone hoe, from New Jersey.
21. Arrowheads, found in Southern States.
            H. J. Tiffin, Esq.
21½. Flint spearhead.   *J. A. Matheson, Jr.*

22. Arrowhead, found at Westmount.
    J. M. Nelson, Esq.
23. Arrowhead, from Isle-du-Pas.   *Louis Julien, Esq.*
24. Stone ball found embedded in Fort Senneville.
    R. A. Campbell, Esq.
25. Arrowheads of the Huron Tribe, found at Brantford, Ont.
26–34. Stone celts, used for skinning animals.
35. Stone gouge.
36. Stone implement.
37. Stone gorget to suspend about the neck.
    Walter Drake, Esq.
38. Three arrowheads from a shell heap, near St. Andrew, N.B.   *R. W. McLachlan, Esq.*
39. Fragment of Indian pottery, "Huron," found at *la Mission Ste-Marie*, by J. C. Tache, Esq.
40. Fragment of Indian pottery, found in a grove at Isle St. Joseph, by J. C. Tache, Esq.   *Hon. Judge Baby.*
41. Two arrowheads, found at Dansville, five miles from Toronto.   *Alfred Sandham, Esq.*
42. Arrowhead, found at Joliette, 1854.
43. Banner-stone, finely polished, found at Joliette, 1854.
    Hon. Judge Baby.
44. Four flint arrowheads, found near Bilbury, England.
    Boswell Belcher, Esq.
45. Small beads of shell, from necklace found at Fraser River, B.C., by Wm. Perry.
    W. D. Lighthall, Esq., K.C.
46. A piece of lignite, found in the Bay des Chaleurs.
    Mrs. J. P. B. Casgrain.
47. Indian tomahawk, found at Owen Sound.
    Thos. O'Leary, Esq.
48. Nail from coffin found in the first Montreal burying ground, St. Paul and St. Nicholas streets.
49. Nails from sacristy of old Bonsecours Church.
    R. W. McLachlan, Esq.
50. Military buttons, found at Fort Isle-aux-Noix.
51. Card. A collection of old military buttons of British Regiments.   *H. J. Tiffin, Esq.*

52. Card. A collection of military buttons, etc., found in and around Fort Isle-aux-Noix.
53. Pieces of old ironwork from the "Giffard Manor" House, at Beauport, Quebec, built in 1634.
  Mrs. Gugy-Ryland.
54. Piece of brick from Fort Missisaga, Niagara, old Fort George.
56. Old powder horn. *Alfred Sandham, Esq.*
57. Old powder horn, inscribed Jonathan French, Swift Packet, London. *W. B. Matheson, Esq.*
58. Old powder horn, picked up on the battlefield at Crysler's Farm, 11th Nov., 1813. *J. Brennan, Esq.*
59. Old powder horn, engraved. *Jno. Riddell, Esq.*
60. Fragments of arrowheads, etc., from lower Manitoulin Island. *J. H. Ross, Esq.*
61. Indian clay pipe, clay bead and bone bodkin, found near Spencerville, Ont. *James Reid, Esq.*
62. Piece of rion and a copper button from Fort Ticonderoga.
  W. D. Lighthall, Esq., K.C.
63. Chip from Nelson's ship Victory. *Dr. Harding.*
64. Indian relic found at Beauharnois.
65. Piece of mortar from the Mountain fort.
66. Human bones from Plains of Abraham.
  J. A. U. Beaudry, Esq.
67. Lead bullet and piece of stone from the Oven of Sieur de Mont's house at Isle-Ste-Croix.
  A. Kleczkowski, Esq.
68. Stone gouge found at Ste. Genevieve de Batiscan. Champlain County. This region was formerly frequented by the Attikameks and the Hurons.
  E. L. Massicotte, Esq.
69. Window frame from a casemate of Fort Isle-aux-Noix.
  Dr. C. Wilson.

METCALFE CHAMBER.

1. The second Borgian Map, by Diego Ribero. Seville, 1529. Fac-simile of the original in the Library of the Vatican, Rome. The first and only time a copy of this map was permitted to be made by the late Pope Leo XIII., for the Columbian Exhibition, at Chicago, 1892. A limited number were published, of which this is one.
  S. C. Stevenson, Esq.

2. Topographical map of Lower Canada, by Samuel Holland, from the Gulf of St. Lawrence up to Quebec, 1810.
Hon. Judge Baby.

3. Champlain, the Explorer. Discoverer of Lake Champlain. *H. J. Tiffin, Esq.*

4. Quebec and vicinity, *in relief* showing the altitude of the land and mountains, the rivers and villages, Island of Orleans, etc. *S. Grant, Esq.*

5. Two Woodcuts. The Crucifixion and St. Peter. These two most interesting prints were found in the Parish Church at Champlain, at the back of two old oil paintings, and are over two hundred years old.
F. E. Meloche, Esq.

6. Christopher Columbus. Discovered America, Oct. 12, 1492. Copy of a portrait in the Royal Museum at Madrid, which bears his autograph.
H. J. Tiffin, Esq.

7. Fac-simile of the list of Jacques-Cartier's crews, preserved in the archives at St. Malo, France.
Hon. Judge Baby.

8. The dispersion of the Acadians, from the painting in St. James' Cathedral.

9. Queen Victoria and her descendants, 1897.

10. Brevet d'Indulgence sent by the Superior of the Recollets in France to Jacques Hervieux, a prominent merchant, Montreal, in 1750. *Madame Lafontaine.*

11. Battle between the Chesapeake and Shannon, the 1st June, 1813.

12. Tiffin. Portrait of H. J. Tiffin, Esq., 1st Vice-President and Life Governor of the Numismatic and Antiquarian Society, one of the founders of the Museum and Library, and who contributed greatly to its success. His donations were innumerable, embracing several hundred rare medals, and many relics to the Museum, many portraits (some in oil), of noted men connected with the past history of Canada; numerous rare and costly steel engravings, etc., etc. He was a generous contributer to the maintenance of the Chateau. Died, March 4, 1903.

13. Old French Windmill and Fort at Vaudreuil.
G. T. Ramsay, Esq.

14. Old door, carved panels, from the Chapel of Notre-Dame-de-la-Victoire, built 1713, demolished 1900.

OLD CANADIAN CHURCHES, ETC.

15. View of the old Church at Boucherville.
16. View of the Church and Village of Varennes.
17. View of St. Ann's Church, at Varennes.
18. View of the old Church at Repentigny.
Hon. Judge Baby.
19. Interior of old Parish Church at Three Rivers.
20. Old Chapel at St. Laurent.
21. Convent, Isle St. Paul.
22. Old Windmill, Vercheres.
23. Working model of one of the first G. T. locomotives running from Montreal to St. Hyacinthe, made by P. Rodier, in 1850, when only fourteen years of age.
Chs. T. Hart, Esq.

COUNCIL ROOM.

1. View of St. Hilaire Mountain, with the cross on its summit erected by Bishop Forbin-Janson, 6th Oct., 1841.
2. Views of Quebec in 1829. 1. Market day in the Upper Town, winter; 2. The old Bishop's Chapel, used as the House of Assembly; 3. Castle St. Louis; 4. Old St. Roch's Church; 5. The General Hospital; 6. The Place d'Armes, in winter; 7. Wolfe and Montcalm monuments; 8. Chapel of the Holy Trinity; 9. Episcopal Church, Point Levis; 10. St. Andrews's Church; 11. English Cathedral; 12. St. John's Capel; 13. The Court House; 14. Methodist Chapel; 15. Quebec from Levis. *G. A. Young, Esq.*
3. View of Quebec, showing the conflagration of June 28, 1845, and the ruins of the fire of May 28, 1845.
By Purchase.
4. *Habitants* playing at cards. Interior of a French-Canadian farmhouse, fifty years ago.
Hon. Judge Baby.
5. The Canadians at Parrderburgh.
H. J. Tiffin, Esq.
.. Chateau St. Louis, Quebec. First built by Champlain, 1635; rebuilt by Frontenac, and destroyed by fire 23rd January, 1834. *H. J. Tiffin, Esq.*
7. British troops on the march in winter from Halifax to Quebec, 1861.

8. Quebec from Point Levi. Colored view showing the Ice Bridge in 1861. *Hon. Judge Baby.*
9. Engagement between the French Frigate *La Surveillante*, commanded by Captain Du Covedic, and the British Frigate, *The Quebec*, Captain Farmer, 6th Oct., 1779.
10. View of the Town and Harbour of Louisbourg, in 1758. View taken near the lighthouse when the city was besieged by Wolfe and Amherst.
11. View of Gaspe Basin, 1758. This French settlement supplied Quebec with fish till it was destroyed by Gen. Wolfe after the surrender of Louisbourg, 1758.
12. View of Perce Rock. A remarkable rock in the Gulf of St. Lawrence. Drawn on the spot by Capt. Hervey Smyth, 1759.
13. View of Halifax, Town and Harbor. Drawn on the spot by Richard Short, 1760.
14. View of Halifax. The Church of St. Paul, and the Parade, by Richard Short, 1760.
15. View of the Town and Harbour of Halifax, east view in 1760.
16. View of Quebec taken from Beauport by Morin, 1851.
17. Plate of 6 colored views of Quebec in 1852: 1. Parliament Buildings; 2. French Cathedral; 3. Monument to Wolfe and Montcalm; 4. St. John's Gate; 5. View of Esplanade; 6. Durham Terrace.
18. Quebec from Point Levis. View taken in 1759, partly from " Pointe-des-Peres " and partly on board the *Vanguard* man-of-war, by Capt. Hervey Smyth.
19. Quebec from Indian Cove. View taken in 1759 by Richard Short.
20. Cape Rouge, nine miles above Quebec. From this place, 1,100 chosen troops, at the break of day, fell down the river, in the ebb tide, to the landing place. 13th Sept., 1759
21. View of Montmorency Falls and the attack made by Wolfe on the French entrenchments, near Beauport with the Grenadiers of the army, July 31, 1759.
22. Stampede of a herd of buffaloes before a prairie fire.
23. Ojibway Indians on the Nepigon.
24. Plan of the Jesuits College at Quebec, rebuilt 1726, demolished 1877. Used for more than a century as a Barracks for British Troops. *Hon. Judge Baby.*

25. View of Quebec. *Very old print.* Belonged to Le Moyne de Longueuil, in 1685.
26. View of the Ice Bridge at Quebec, in 1832.
27. Fac-simile of card of invitation to attend the funeral of Sir Wm. Phipps, Thursday, 21st Feb., 1694. Phipps was defeated before Quebec by Frontenac, in 1690.
28. Death of General Wolfe on the Plains of Abraham, 13th Sept., 1759.
Painted by B. West. Engraved by W. Woollett.
29. Death of General the Marquis de Montcalm, 13th Sept., 1759.
30. Contemporary copy in oil of the portrait of Benjamin Franklin in the Uffizi Gallery, Florence.
James Morgan, Esq.
31. A letter written in the Chateau in 1776 and signed by the three Commissioners of Congress,—B. Franklin, Saml. Chase and Chs. Carroll of Carrollton.
By Purchase.
32. Plan of the Battle of the Plains of Abraham, with twelve views of churches, etc., in Quebec, showing the effect of the bombardment, in 1759. *Very rare.*
T. O'Leary, Esq.
33. Plan of the Operations of the British Army before Quebec in 1759. Published by Alfred Hawkins in 1846. *Rare.* *R. B. Angus, Esq.*
34. View of the ice bridge before Quebec in 1832. By Lieut.-Col. Cockburn. *Hon. Judge Baby.*
35. Quebec, from below d'Aubigny Church, Point Levi. From a drawing by Lieut.-Col. Cockburn, dedicated to His Majesty William IV., 1833. *Hon. Judge Baby.*
36. Quebec and Lower Town, from the Citadel, shows the old castle St. Louis, 1833. *Hon. Judge Baby.*
37. View of Wolfe's Cove and Cape Diamond from Sillery Heights, by Col. Cockburn. *Hon. Judge Baby.*
38. The Ice Cone at Montmorency Falls, as it appeared in 1829, by Col. Cockburn. *Hon. Judge Baby.*
39. View of Port of Quebec *Old French print*, purely imaginative, but very interesting.
40. View of the Lower Town of Quebec, in 1759.
41. View in the Upper Town, Quebec, 1759.
42. View of the Place Royale, Lower Town, Quebec, 1759.

43. View of the Recollets, in the Upper Town, 1759.
44. Ruins of the Castle St. Louis, Quebec. From a sketch made by the Rev. E. Sewell, shortly after the fire, 1834.
Wm. de Quincy Sewell, Esq.
45. View of the Seigniory of Chambly.
Mr. Joyce, Chambly.
46. View of the Village of Chambly in 1830.
Mr. Joyce, Chambly.
47. View of Esplanade and Fortifications, Quebec, in 1832.
48. Upper Town, Market and Parish Church, Quebec, in 1832.
49. View of the Place-d'Armes and Episcopal Cathedral, Quebec, in 1832. *J. Snedden, Esq.*
50. Quebec from Point Levis. View taken, 1832.
J. Snedden, Esq.
51. Habitant going to market in the old days. *Sketch by Henri Julien.*
52. Dollard and his companions at the Long-Sault, May, 1660, *by Henri Julien. Emile Vaillancourt, Esq.*
53. Old Windmill at Lachine. *E. Lucas, Esq.*
54. Chateau St. Louis, Quebec. *Vide* No. 6. Pen and ink sketch by the donor. *Thos. O'Leary, Esq.*
55. A chronological table of the Governors and Administrators of Canada from its first settlement to 17th Oct., 1850. From the *Album de Souvenirs* of Lt.-Col. Jacques Viger, first Mayor of Montreal.
56. Calendar for the City and District of Quebec, for the year 1799. *Hon. Judge Baby.*
57. Illustrations from the donor's book, "The Habitant," showing scenes from Canadian life.
Dr. W. H. Drummond
58. Quebec, from below d'Aubigny Church, Point Levi. From a drawing by Lieut.-Col. Cockburn, dedicated to His Majesty William IV., 1833. *Hon. Judge Baby.*
59. View of the O'Leary models of the historic gates of Quebec. These models are perfect fac-similes of the old gates and surroundings, now in the Library of McGill University. *F. W. Wurtele, Esq.*
60. Interior view of Old Fort Garry, a vanished scene.

61. Flag of the Patriots, carried in the Insurrection of 1837.
    Victor Morin, Esq.
62. Making maple syrup. A scene in the Canadian woods.
    Hon. Judge Baby.
63. Siege of Louisburg in 1745. *R. W. McLachlan, Esq.*
64. View of the oldest church in America. In Greenland, A.D., 980. *H. J. Tiffin, Esq.*
65. Lord Elgin closing the Canadian Parliament in 1853.
    H. J. Tiffin, Esq.
66. The Town and Fortification of Louisburg, in 1745.
    Thos. O'Leary, Esq.

ANTIQUITIES.

67. Halberd. An antique halberd dug up on the bank of Little River Lairet, Quebec, 1841. On this spot Jacques Cartier wintered in 1535. *Hon. Judge Baby.*
68. Old Canadian axe, 1660.
69. Old flint-lock musket. Made the campaign of the Revolutionary War in the States, 1775-1786, and was used for hunting purposes for many years in the State of New York. *Rev. L. N. St. Onge.*
70. Old flint-lock musket, used by a British soldier during Revolutionary War, 1775.
71. Old "Brown Bess" musket, picked up on the battlefield of Chrysler's Farm, 11th Nov., 1813.
    J. Brennan, Esq.
72. Old flint-lock musket, used in the battle of Chateauguay, 1813. *W. A. Scott, Esq.*
73. Needle-gun. Franco-Prussian War, 1870.
    James Milloy, Esq.
74. Fenian rifle, taken at Trout River, 1870.
    G. H. Dalgleish, Esq.
75. Old flint-lock musket and bayonet carried in 1837 by the late Wm. Francis, Esq.
76. Old flint-lock musket, having two locks but one barrel.
    Hon. Judge Baby.
77. Flint-lock, never in use, found in the stock of a hardware store on St. Paul Street, 1895. *G. H. Matthews, Esq.*
78. Winchester rifle, found on the prairies in the North-West, used in Riel's Rebellion. *C. Chapman, Esq.*

79. High Constable's baton. Time of George III. Used in the Court House, Montreal. *Natural History Society.*
80. Antique carved table, made from wood carving of the old Parish Church, Montreal. *C. H. Catelli, Esq.*
81. Model of the old Bonsecours Church. Perfect facsimile of the old church before it underwent the socalled restoration. *Hon. Judge Baby.*
82. Fanlight of a window from the Chapel of Notre-Dame de la Victoire, built 1713; demolished in 1900.

CASE 1.

RELICS.

1. Hat worn by Louis Riel at the battle of Batoche, 12th May, 1885, and given by him to one of the counsel for his defence.
2. Wooden hand. Part of a statue which was over the door of the Parish Church, on Place-d'Armes.
 Seminary of St. Sulpice.
3. Photograph of the steamboat *Beaver*, the first steamer on the North Pacific; wrecked near Vancouver, in 1892; also, pieces of a hawser, wood, copper, etc., from her hull.
 Saulter, Esq.
4. Piece of a beam from the ruins of Fort Senneville, built 1690; dismantled, 1775.
5. A section of a wooden pipe of the first waterworks of Montreal, 1801 to 1815. *G. H. Matthews, Esq.*
6. Antique coffee urn found in the vaults of the old Seminary, Montreal. *Hon. Judge Baby.*
7. Chief's war club, from one of the South Pacific Islands.
8. Brick from the foundation wall of the Chateau de Ramezay.

CASE 2.

BOER RELICS.

1. Bird's nest from the Modder River.
2. 6 Cartridges (Boer) from Douglass.
3. Pebble from Fourteen Streams.
4. Clippers from Boer house, Faber's Farm.
5. Piece of shell from Fourteen Streams.
 The donor was a member of the Royal Canadian Artillery, 2nd Contingent, South Africa.
 Real Huot, Esq.

6. Boer Hat picked up 14 miles from Johannesburg. The donor was a member of Brabant's Scouts.
Alfred Brown, Esq.
7. Piece of Boer shell.
8. Water bottle.
9. Revolver.
10. Sword-bayonet.
11. Piece of bomb. *Eug. A. Globensky, Esq.*
12. Zulu's bead necklace.
13. Zulu's bead belt. *Mrs. W. R. Salter.*
14. Horse saddle, made by an early settler.
15. Three rivets from the centre span of the old Victoria Bridge, Dec. 10, 1898. *Dr. W. G. Nichol.*
16. Rivet from the old Victoria Bridge.
Arthur Baby, Esq.
17. Rivets from the old Victoria Bridge.
The donor's father, Major Campbell, accompanied H.R.H. the Prince of Wales across the bridge, 1860.
Colin Campbell, Esq.
18. Ring-bolt, from the first French prison of Montreal to which condemned murderers were chained.
Hon. Judge Baby.
19. Old iron implement, dredged up in the harbor of Montreal. *C. de B. Leprohon, Esq.*
20. Old iron implement, found in excavating the cellar of an old French house on Notre Dame Street.
Alphonse Goree, Esq.
21. Iron lamp, in use in the country districts fifty years ago.
Thos. O'Leary, Esq.
22. Old iron lamp used in Scotland 150 years ago, brought to Canada, in 1810, by Wm. McGibbon, of Dundee, Quebec. *Andrew Taylor, Esq.*
23. Old rion lamp, from officers' quarters, Fort Chambly, 1812.
24. A piece of the cornice of the southwest door of the Jesuits' College, Quebec. *Hon. Judge Baby.*

CASE 3.

PHOTOGRAPHS.
1. Squerryes Court, Westerham, Kent, Eng. The residence of the Wardes of Squerryes. Wolfe's young friends. *Col. and the Hon. Mrs. Warde.*

2. Banner preserved at Oka. Made in 1752 to commemorate a treaty with the Indians.
Rev. Ls. St. Jean.
3. Old Block-house, Philipsburgh.
W. D. Lighthall, Esq., K.C.
4. Ruins of Fort Senneville, with the President and members of the Antiquarian Society.
Lapres & Lavergne.
5. Old French house, de Vaudreuil Street, in the vaults of which the "Montreal Bank" stored the specie in its early years, 1817. *Hon. Judge Baby.*
6. Pres-de-Ville. Country house of Le Moyne de Maricour, now Cote Street. *W. D. Lighthall, Esq., K.C.*
7. Ruins of Chateau Bigot, Charlesbourg, near Quebec.
Miss Alice Baker.
8. Ruins of the Intendant's Palace, Quebec.
Miss Alice Baker.
9. The oldest French house in Laprairie. *Dr. Brisson.*
10. Old Windmill at St. Ann's. *Lapres & Lavergne.*
11. Old Block-house at Philipsburgh in 1898.
12. Two views of "*La Friponne,*" Bigot's old store house.
13. Unveiling of the Chateauguay Monument, on the anniversary of the battle, Oct. 26, 1895.
14. Wolfe and Montcalm Monument, Quebec. *Photo by the donor.* *W. D. Lighthall, Esq., K.C.*

CASE 4.

PHOTOGRAPHS.

1. Part of Fort (interior), Caughnawaga.
2. Books of the old French Jesuits and Pere La Jeunne's portrait in the presbytery.
3. Church, Presbytery and Fortifications, built in 1721.
4. Presbytery, 1721.
5. Old loop-holed house, within the fortifications.
6. Chamber and desk of Pere Charlevoix, where he wrote part of his history of la Nouvelle France, 1725.
7. Parish Church of Sandy Bay.
8. Chapel of one of the old towers of *le "Fort de la Montagne."*

9. The Island and Nunnery. Chateauguay Basin.
10. Old house at the deserted Cedars Canal.
11. The oldest church in Canada, at Tadousac.
    Nos. 1 to 11 photographed by J. G. Ross, Esq.
          W. D. Lighthall, Esq., K.C.
12. Le Fort de la Montagne.
13. Sketch of the Chateau de Ramezay in 1849, by the donor.   *W. B. Lamb, Esq.*
14. Photograph of gold medal presented by the citizens of Quebec to Ludger Duvernay, on his release from prison, in 1832.
15. Photograph of gold medal presented by the citizens of Montreal, to Ludger Duvernay, on his release from prison, in 1832.
16. Photograph of the de Salaberry "Chateauguay" gold medal, 1812, presented to him by the Legislative of Lower Canada.
17. Photograph of the Beaver Club medal.
18. Four views of the ruins of Fort Ticonderoga, May 24, 1897.   *Hon. Judge Baby.*

CASE 5.

1. Gold epaulettes worn by a French-Canadian officer during the War of 1812.
2. Gilt chain epaulettes worn by an officer in the Canadian Militia, during the American Invasion, 1775.
          H. J. Tiffin, Esq.
3. Epaulettes worn by Capt. McBride, R.E., 1832.
          James Milloy, Esq.
4. Regalia. Collars of the President, First and Second Vice-Presidents of St. Jean Baptiste Society when founded by Ludger Duvernay, in 1834.
          By Purchase.
5. Masonic apron of Col. Jonathan Odell, founder of Odelltown. U.E.L. officer of Militia in War of 1812.
          Mrs. Lt.-Col. McEachren.
6. Rosette worn at the funeral of the Hon. D'Arcy McGee, Montreal, April 13, 1868.
          W. D. Lighthall, Esq., K.C.
7. Cannon ball found in cellar of old house, 61 St. Paul Street.   *P. O. Tremblay, Esq.*

8. A four pound cannon ball found in an excavation on ramparts at Quebec in 1860 by the donor.
J. A. U. Beaudry, Esq.

9. Cannon ball found at Boucherville.
L. N. Pare, Esq.

10. Cannon ball found embedded in a sand bank at Three Rivers. *Joseph Raynor, Esq.*

11. Cannon ball (battle of St. Denis) found embedded in the wall of an old house. *Rev. L. N. St. Onge,*

12. Cannon ball, 12 pounder, from battle of Schuylerville or Saratoga, fought Oct., 1777, found in the crevice of a quarry, in 1800. *Rev. L. N. St. Onge.*

13. Cannon ball, 24 pounder, from the Plains of Abraham, stamped with the *fleur-de-lis*. *Dr. Louis Laberge.*

14. Three cannon balls and crowbar from the French ship *La Prudente*, sunk in the Harbor of Louisburg, in 1758.
Messrs. Reid & Co., Quebec.

15. Cannon ball from *La Prudente*, 1758.
S. Coulson, Esq.

15. Cannon ball from *La Prudente*, 1758.
S. Coulson, Esq.

16. Caronade ball found on Logan's farm in 1887.

17. Grape shot dug up at Montmorency Falls.

18. Cannon ball dredged up in the Harbor of Montreal.
Henry Mott, Esq.

19. Cannon ball from the battlefield of St. Charles, 1837
L. H. Hebert, Esq.

20. Bar-shot used in the siege of Quebec.
Rev. J. D. Borthwick.

21. The military coat worn by Adjutant James Miller, who organized several of the Canadian Militia corps during the war of 1812. *Robert Miller, Esq.*

22. The military coat and sword of Captain Dumais, a Canadian officer of Militia during the American Invasion of Canada, 1775-6. *W. D. Lighthall, Esq.*

23. Coat worn by a private of the Canadian Militia in 1837.
Mrs. Cushing.

24. Cocked hat or *Chapeau*, worn by Surgeon Heriot of the King's Carbineers, in the Peninsular War and at Waterloo. *J. C. Heriot, Esq.*

25. Tunic worn by John Sandfield Macdonald, when Colonel of a Canadian Infantry Regiment in 1838, with silver epaulettes. *Geo. Sandfield Macdonald, Esq.*

OBSERVE.—The stone mantel and grate in this room were formerly in the building commonly known as "de Beaujeu" house, but built by Col. Campbell, who had married a Miss de Chapt de Lacorne de St. Luc. This property originally belonged to Jean-Baptiste-Nicolas Roch de Ramezay, son of Governor Claude de Ramezay. In 1759 he was commandant of Quebec and signed the capitulation of that city to the British.
The Heirs de Beaujeu.

THE ANTE-ROOM.

1. Antique pianoforte made by Longman, Clementi and Company, Cheapside, London, 1775, and which belonged to the de Lorimier family, at l'Assomption.
Hon. Judge Baby.

2. Piano. This piano was one of the very first manufactured in Montreal, about 1805. *F. J. Granger, Esq.*

3. Oak table made from a beam of Tower of the old Notre Dame Church. *Mrs. A. K. Gregor.*

4. Campaign Desk of Count de Malartic, an officer in the Regiment of Bearne, and secretary to Gen. Montcalm, 1754-60. *Hon. Judge Baby.*

5. A box, made in oak, for holding documents, belonged to Jean-Claude Panet, the first of that name in Canada, 1745. *Hon. Judge Baby.*

6. The military campaign dressing-case of General Thomas Gage, first English Governor of Montreal, 1760.
Hon. Judge Baby.

7. Barrel Organ, presented by George III. to Thayendanegea, the celebrated Chief of the Six Nations.
H. H. Date, Esq.

8. Thayendanegea (Joseph Brant). A celebrated Indian Chief of pure Mohawk blood, chief of the Six Nations Was highly educated, and visited England on several occasions. Died in 1807, aged 65 years.
Hon. Judge Baby.

9. Huron Chiefs. Three chiefs who were presented at Court, 7th April, 1823.

10. Vincent Nicholas (*Tsawanhonhi*). Principal chief of the Hurons at Lorette who was presented to His Majesty George IV., 7th April, 1823. *By Subscription.*

11. Forty-three portraits and Camp Scenes of Indians of the Dominion North-West.
 C. T. Hart and W. D. Lighthall, Esq., K.C.

12. Moose hunting in Canada—2 views

13. The March of Miles Standish. *Dr. W. G. Nichol*

14. The Last Great Council of the West. From the original painting in the possession of the Marquis of Lorne.
 Painted by Sydney P. Hall. *H. J. Tiffin, Esq.*

15. The last of the Red Skins, Indians pursued by U.S. Cavalry.

THE SALON.

Scene of the Receptions of the French and British Regimes. In this room General Montgomery met the citizens of Montreal in 1775, as also did Benj. Franklin, Carroll of Carrollton, and Samuel Chase, in 1776.

OBSERVE.—The very spacious old fire-place, used for log fires in the olden time.

The wood mantel was in the house built by Baron de Becancour, in 1720, and occupied by the late Hon. James McGill for many years.

A. Massive mahogany sofa. Belonged to Lord Sydenham, Governor-General of Canada, 1839. *By Purchase.*

B. Iron plate. One of the first castings after the conquest, date 1763, was placed in the wall of the old Montreal College. *H. R. Ives, Esq.*

C. Antique English Clock, which belonged to the Hon. James McGill, 1793.

D. Antique clock which belonged to Marie-Anne Hervieux, daughter of Pierre Hervieux and Charlotte Marie de la Margne, and wife of J.-Bte.-Melchior Hertel de Rouville, 10th May, 1784. *Hon. Judge Baby.*

E. Bust of Hon. L. H. Holton, a prominent Montreal merchant and statesman. *J. B. Learmont, Esq.*

F. Model of a Quebec timber ship, 1859.

G. Model of a British steam corvette, 1856.

H. Case containing a number of models of boats, canoes, cayaks, etc.,—as used by the Esquimaux.
 Loaned by C. T. Hart, Esq.

I. Case containing samples of Canadian handicraft work.

MONTREAL VIEWS.

1. Birds eye view of the City of Montreal, 1889.
By Purchase.
2. The first Victoria Bridge. Summer and winter view. Cost six million dollars, was opened by H.R.H. the then Prince of Wales, in 1860. The tube was removed in 1899 and replaced by trusses. *Dr. W. G. Nichol.*
3. Ten views of Montreal in 1870.
1. Great St. James St.; 2. English Cathedral; 3. McGill College; 4. Harbor, looking west; Victoria Bridge; 6. Montreal from the Mountain; 7. Harbor east; 8. Court House; 9. French Parish Church; 10. Victoria Square. *R. W. McLachlan, Esq.*
4. Catalognes Plan of Ville Marie in 1723.
5. View of the Town of Montreal in Canada, 1760.
E. L. Bond, Esq.
6. View of the City of Montreal from the Mountain, 1870.
7. Very rare view of Montreal, in 1784. View taken from the Mountain showing the Fortifications, Chateau, Jesuit's Church, etc. Photographed from the original in the British Museum by the donor.
George H. W. Birch, Esq.
8. Illustrations from "Hochelaga Depicta," or History of Montreal, 1832.
9. 10. Two oil paintings. Montreal from St. Helen's Island, and Montreal from the Mountain in 1838. Painted that year by J. Duncan for the Bank of Montreal.
Presented to the Chateau by A. E. Adams, Esq.
11. Large view of Montreal in 1851, looking from the Mountain, oil painting by J. Murray.
The Misses Dow.
12. View of the Place-d'Armes and French Cathedral, 1832.
13. Notre-Dame Street, Montreal, in 1830.
14. View of St. James Street, Montreal, in 1830.
15. View of Notre-Dame Street, looking east from McGill, 1830. *G. A. Young, Esq.*
16. Plan of the Town and Fortifications of Montreal in 1768. Copied from the original plan of the Royal Engineers in the Dominion Archives.
Presented by George H. W. Birch, Esq.

17, 18, 19. Three views of the old McGill house, corner Jacques-Cartier Square and Notre-Dame Street. Built in 1720 by Baron de Becancour; demolished in 1903. This house was occupied by the late Hon. James McGill for many years. Sketched by donor.
R. G. Matthews, Esq.

20. Colored view of Montreal, from the Mountain, 1870.
Alfred Sandham, Esq.

21. Panoramic view of the Harbor of Montreal from Victoria Bridge to below the jail, 1861.
Thos. Urban Herst, Esq.

22. Duncan's Panoramic view of Montreal, from St. Helen's Island in 1847. *G. Alfred Pelland, Esq.*

23. Plan of Montreal in 1760. *R. B. Angus, Esq.*

24. Oil painting of the old mill at Windmill Point, painted by Hawksett. *James Morgan, Esq.*

25. Funeral procession of the late Hon. Thomas D'Arcy McGee, April 13, 1869. *View taken on St. James Street.*
S. M. Baylis, Esq.

26. Montreal from the Mountain. Water color by Duncan, 1856. *J. Wolferstan Thomas, Esq.*

27. Montreal from the Mountain, view taken in 1850.
J. Wolferstan Thomas, Esq.

28. View of the City of Montreal in 1855, drawn by E. Whitefield. *Albert Lewis, Esq.*

29. View of Montreal from St. Helen's Island, 1875, by J. Duncan.

30. East view of Montreal in 1807, *by Richard Dillon.*

31. Old French windmill, which stood between St. Lawrence and St. Dominique streets, near the present St. Hypolite street. *Hon. Judge Baby.*

32. View of Place d'Armes and Bank of Montreal in 1850, (a very rare colored print.) *Hon. Judge Baby.*

33. A view of the City of Montreal and the River St. Lawrence from the Mountain *by E. Walsh, 49th Reg't,* 1810.
By Purchase.

BOURNE'S VIEWS.

34. View of the Champ de Mars, 1830.

35. View of Montreal from the Island, 1830.

36. St. James Street in 1830.
37. Place d'Armes, Montreal, 1830.
38. View of the Harbour, Montreal, 1830.
39. View of Montreal from the Island, in 1760, *old print.*
Hon. Judge Baby.
40. Chateau Callieres, built by Governor Callieres in 1683, demolished 1780.
41. Old Parish Church of Notre Dame, Montreal, built in 1672, removed in 1830. *Mrs. J. R. Thibaudeau.*
42. View of Bout-de-l'Isle, Montreal, in winter, after a painting by Kreighoff, 1850. *Hon. Judge Baby.*
43. Place d'Armes, Montreal, in 1807. *Photograph of Dillon's view.* *Wm. McLellan, Esq.*
44. Burning of the Anglican Cathedral, Notre Dame St., on the night of Tuesday, December 9, 1856.
Judge L. W. Sicotte.
45. The Bishop's Palace, corner of St. Catherine and St. Denis streets, destroyed in the great fire of 1852.
J. A. U. Beaudry, Esq.
46. A Winter fire in Montreal. Burning of stores on St. James street. *Dr. W. G. Nichol.*
47. Bonaventure Depot, great flood of 1867.
48. Photograph of Duncan's painting of the funeral of Gen'l d'Urban.
49. Christ Church Cathedral, Montreal.
G. W. Sadler, Esq.
50. View of Montreal from the Mountain *by R. S. M. Bouchette*, 1831.
51. View of the Old Grey Nunnery on McGill Street.
By Purchase.
52. View of the Old Recollet Church and Convent on Notre Dame Street. *By Purchase.*
55. Parish Church and Place d'Armes in 1805.
By Purchase.

WEST HALL.

1. Antique oak Flemish chest, 16th century.
H. J. Tiffin, Esq.
2. Two old military chairs. Were in the Royal Engineers' Office, 1847. *W. D. Lighthall, Esq., K.C.*

3. Large piece of Gobelin Tapestry, Court amusements in the time of Louis XIV.
H. J. Tiffin and James Morgan, Esq.

THE LOUIS XIV. ROOM.

The restoration of this room has been done by the Woman's Branch of the Antiquarian Society. The style is of the time of Louis XIV., it being that king who appointed de Ramezay Governor of Montreal.

1. The arms of Louis XIV. Tapestry after Le Brun, 1680. Charles Le Brun, first painter to the King, director of the manufactures at the Gobelins, director and rector of the Royal Academy of Painting and Sculpture, born 1618, died 1690. Louis XIV. presented the artist with his miniature set with diamonds, and granted him letters of *noblesse*. One of the Le Brun's paintings is in the Basilica, Quebec.

2. Johnson, Sir William, of Johnson Hall, in the Mohawk Valley. Major-General of the New York militia. Born in Ireland, 1714. Came to America, 1734. Had great influence over the Iroquois. In 1759 he commanded under Gen. Prideaux in the expedition against Fort Niagara. Died, 1774. *H. J. Tiffin, Esq.*

3. Colbert, Jean-Baptiste. A financial statesman, born in 1619. Louis XIV. made him comptroller-general of finances. He extended the colonial power of France. He died in 1683.

4. La Salle presenting his petition to Louis XIV. in presence of Colbert. *H. J. Tiffin, Esq.*

5. Antique mahogany cabinet. Belonged to Guy Carleton, Lord Dorchester, Governor-General of Canada, 1767 to 1777. *Woman's Branch.*

6. Antique crystal chandlier. Belonged to the Baby family. Hung in the house of the Hon. Frs. Baby, at Quebec, in 1782. *Hon. Judge Baby.*

7. Old Colonial chair. Belonged to one of Fraser's Highlanders who settled at Murray Bay, below Quebec, in 1760. *Dr. Louis Laberge.*

8. A Louis XV. chair. Belonged to the Marquis de Lotbiniere, 1740. *Mme de B. Macdonald.*

9. Antique sofa of the time of Governor de Vaudreuil, 1723.
Woman's Branch.

10. Old Canadian chair, 1780. *Hon. Judge Baby.*
11. The arms of the Marquis de Lotbiniere in tapestry, the work of the donor. *Mme de B. Macdonald.*
12. Antique urn, in Rhine stone, which was for a long time in the possession of the Aubert de Gaspe family.
Hon. Judge Baby.
13. Two brass candlesticks. Were in the house at Sorel that was for a time the residence of the Duke of Kent.
Mme de B. Macdonald.
14. Portrait of the late Mme de B. Macdonald, President of the Woman's Antiquarian Society.
Painted by R. G. Mathews.
15. Oil painting, by Many Benner, of a young girl symbolical of the Province of Alsace, lost to France in 1870. Presented to the Chateau by the Minister of War, through M. L. Herbette, Councillor of State, who represented France at the Quebec Tercentenary, 1908.
16. A Louis XV. Commode tulip wood and Kings wood, with brass mounts and marble top, a family relic from a Chateau in France.
Loaned by W. D. Lighthall, Esq., K.C.

THE HABITANT ROOM.

The arrangement of this room represents the living-room in a Canadian farmhouse, having the same style of chairs, bed, rag carpet (catalogne), etc., usually seen there.

1. Old grandfather's clock. This clock belonged to an old French-Canadian family at Caughnawaga, later it became the property of one of the Indian chiefs.
H. J. Tiffin, Esq.
2. Old arm chair, one hundred and fifty years old. Belonged to an old Canadian family.
Hon. Judge Baby.
3. Three old Canadian chairs. Belonged to the Beaubien family in 1767. *Messrs. Tiffin and Baby.*
4. Old settle-bed. This style of bed was in common use until recent years. It was used as a seat in day time.
Lady Lacoste.
5. Old spinning-wheel. This wheel is two hundred years old. It belonged to the late Mrs. Bourgeoies, of St. Marcel. She got it from her grandmother, Josephine Littlefield, who was one of the captives brought from New England, about 1703, and adopted by a Canadian family who had ransomed her from the Indians. Later she refused to return to her own people.
Rev. L. N. St. Onge.

6. Old French musket. Belonged to the d'Ailleboust family at l'Assomption. *Hon. Judge Baby.*

7. Old earthenware water cooler of a hundred and fifty years ago. *Mme Horace Baby.*

8. Wooden candlesticks, belonged to the Chateau Chapel.

9, 10, and 11. An ancient cupboard, chest of drawers, and a chair. Furniture of Old Canada, 1754-60.

12. A very old cupboard or *Armoire Canadienne.* *Hon. Judge Baby.*

13. A *Huche Canadienne*, or bread-trough, and oaken bucket. *Mme Veuve Liard.*

14. Two very old Canadian chairs, 1787.

15. Band-box made of birch bark, in use in 1780, for bolding bonnets.

16. Britannia ware teapot. Belonged to the family of the Hon. B. Joliette, 1824.

17. Antique French mirror. Belonged to the family of Dandonneau du Sable, 1704.

18. A very old mirror from the de Lorimier family at l'Assomption, P.Q. *Hon. Judge Baby.*

19. A very curious combination chair and table. Was in use for over seventy years in a French-Canadian farm house.

20. Very old arm chair. Was for a great many years in the church of l'Ange-Gardien, below Quebec.

21. A Jocobean table. Rarely to be found in Canada. From the vestry of an old Canadian church. *W. D. Lighthall, Esq., K.C.*

22. A Canadian bed-quilt. Made by a farmer's wife. *Mme R. Roy.*

23. St. Fereol, Cote de Beaupre. Colored view, after a painting by Kreighoff. *C. T. Hart, Esq.*

24. Very old arm chair, from the chapel of the Huron Indians at Lorette, near Quebec.

25. Old Canadian habitant chair. *W. D. Lighthall, Esq., K.C.*

26. An old Canadian loom, such as used by the French Canadian farmers' wives in making *Catalognes*, bed spreads, homespuns, etc., etc. *Mrs. R. Hemsley.*

27. An old time foot warmer used by the early settlers in going to meeting.

28. An Antique Italian Crimping Iron. *Miss Davidson.*
29. An Eskimo Kayak from the Arctic.
Mrs. L. W. Sicotte.

THE VAULTS.

No. 1.

In this vault the first printing press in Montreal was set up, in 1776, by Mesplets, who accompanied Benjamin Franklin and the other two envoys who had been sent by Congress in the spring of that year. Mesplets, a Frenchman, remained in Montreal after the Americans withdrew. He opened a printing office on Place Royale, where he published the *Montreal Gazette.*

No. 2.

1. In this vault may be seen an ancient *Caleche*, which was the most stylish vehicle in the olden time.

2. Old scales. Belonged to the French Jesuits, and dates to 1683. They were used in a mill at Cap de la Madeleine, near Three Rivers. *T. Lefebvre, Esq.*

3. The Rigaud Bell. This Bell was cast in London in 1801 for the parish church at Rigaud, where it was in use for many years. *C. de Lery Macdonald, Esq.*

4. A wooden pipe of the first water-works in Montreal, 1801-1815. *— Starke, Esq*

5. The weather-vane from old St. Gabriel Church, the first Protestant church built in Montreal, 1792; demolished, 1903.

6. A very finely wrought weather-vane from one of the out buildings of the Chateau.

7. Iron knee of the King's ship *l'Original*, which sank in the harbor of Quebec, in 1750, while being launched.
Quebec Harbor Commissioners.

8. Old crane, from an early French house on Jacques Cartier Square. *F. D. Monk, Esq.*

9. A panel from the Chapel of Notre-Dame-de-Victoire, built, 1713; demolished, 1900. *W. D. Lighthall, Esq., K.C.*

10. A piece of oak planking of the steamboat *John Bull*, one of the first steamboats on the St. Lawrence.
L. N. Pare, Esq.

11. A piece of a beam from the Gobert house, Quebec, in which Gen. Montgomery's body was laid, 1st Jan., 1776.
P. Poulin, Esq.

12. A piece of cornice of a room in the old McGill house 1720-1903.

13. The first fire-engine sent out to Montreal by the Phoenix Fire Insurance Company, in 1805.
Alex. T. Patterson, Esq.

14. A piece of rail of the first railroad in Canada between Montreal and St. John's, 1836.

15. Piece of oak of man-of-war sunk in the River Richelieu in front of Fort St. John by Gen. Montgomery in 1775.
P. J. L'Heureux, Esq.

16. Lord Durham's carrige, brought from England by him when Governor-General of Canada, 1838.
Dr. John Johnson.

17. Ring-bolt from first English Prison, Montreal, 1803.
Sheriff Lemieux.

No. 3.

This vault in the olden time, was used for storage purposes. It was divided into four parts by walls about four feet in thickness, two of which were removed. During the occupancy by the English Governors, this vault was used as a wine cellar.

No. 4.

This vault was the principal kitchen of the Chateau. The great fire-place had a crane on which the pots were hung and up the chimney is an iron rod on which hams and bacon were smoked. A recess at the side is where a wheel was used in turning the spit, and generally worked by a dog.

No. 5.

This vault was used as a kitchen and bakery. In the side of the fire-place is the capacious oven, in as perfect condition as when in use two centuries ago.

THE LAWN.

In front of the Chateau, is the Louisbourg Gun, weighing four tons. This gun was on the French man-of-war *La Prudente*, which was sunk by the English in the harbor of Louisbourg, in 1758. It was raised in 1900, brought to Montreal, and presented to the Chateau by
S. Coulson, Esq.

The gun carriage—an old English one of oak, made in 1843—was presented by Sir Frederick W. Borden
Minister of Militia.

The pile of solid shot number 91. This shot was brought from Cuba after the Spanish-American War.
R. W. McLachlan, Esq.

Cannon from one of the nine ships of Sir Hovenden Walker's fleet, wrecked on *Isle-aux-Oeufs*, Aug. 26, 1711, in the expedition which sailed for Quebec to wrest Canada from the French. *Geo. Boulter, Esq.*

The front tower of the Chateau is surmounted by an antique wrought-iron vane (from the old Recollet Church, Notre Dame Street), made in 1692.

On the rear tower of the Chateau is the Cross of the Recollet Church, 1692. *Hon. Judge Baby.*

Date Due

Souvenirs of the Chateau
MAY BE OBTAINED AT THE COUNTER

VISITORS should not fail to procure some of these Souvenirs. They are intrinsically interesting and valuable, and are sold for the   .·   .·

BENEFIT OF THE CHATEAU

A National Pride.   Popular Everywhere.   Made in Canada.   "The Best."

GURD'S GINGER ALE .· .·
CALEDONIA WATER, ETC.

Under direct management of Mr. Charles Gurd since 1868.
In purchasing please see that our label is on every bottle as this is a guarantee against inferior substitutes.   .·   .·   .·   .·

CHARLES GURD & COMPANY, LIMITED
76 BLEURY STREET, MONTREAL

The Montreal City and District Savings Bank
INCORPORATED 1846

Capital Subscribed $2,000,000   Capital paid up $1,000,000   Reserve Fund $1,150,000
Hon. J. Ald. Ouimet, Pres.   A. P. Lesperance, Mgr.
TOTAL ASSETS OVER $30,000,000   NUMBER OF DEPOSITORS OVER 100,000

The Only Bank Incorporated under the Savings Bank Act, doing business in the City of Montreal. Its Charter (different from all other banks) is so framed to give all possible protection to its depositors.   .·   .·   .·   .·   .·   .·

MICROCOPY RESOLUTION TEST CHART

(ANSI and ISO TEST CHART No 2)

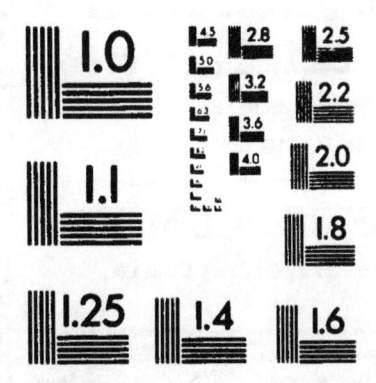

APPLIED IMAGE Inc
1653 East Main Street
Rochester, New York 14609 USA
(716) 482 – 0300 – Phone
(716) 288 – 5989 – Fax

Old Mahogany and Rosewood Furniture
In Rare Old

CHIPPENDALE, SHERATON and COLONIAL

Old Silver and Sheffield Plate,
Quaint Old Brass and Copper,
Rare China and Bric-a-Brac,
Grandfather and Mantel Clocks

We extend a special invitation to visit our

Antique Art Galleries

Phillips Square, MONTREAL

Tel. Up. 1076

B. M. & T. JENKINS, LIMITED
424 Yonge Street, Toronto

THE HERALD PRESS
at MONTREAL

CPSIA information can be obtained
at www.ICGtesting.com
Printed in the USA
BVHW060931041218
534639BV00018BA/735/P